THE FLOWER ESSENCE JOURNAL

Issue #4

Editor / Richard Katz
Associate Editor / Patricia Kaminski
Artists / Pamela Beesley, Catalina, Niki Broyles, Entéra, Penelope Hoblin, David Sherrod,
    Maitreya Stillwater, John Tingley
Photography / Steve Koke, Larry Miller, Michael Pinter, David Siegler
Typesetting / Dwan Typography, Nevada City, California
Printing / Blue Dolphin Press, Grass Valley, California

The Flower Essence Journal is published annually by Gold Circle Productions, P.O. Box 586, Nevada City, CA 95959, USA for the Flower Essence Society, P.O. Box 459, Nevada City, CA 95959, USA (916) 265-9163. Prices for this issue: single copies: $7.00 each; 5-49 copies: $4.20 each (40% discount); 50 or more copies: $3.15 each (55% discount). Copyright © 1982 by the Flower Essence Society. All rights reserved. This issue originally published August, 1982.

ISSN 0732-8389
ISBN 0-943986-04-4

FLOWER ESSENCES are prepared from diluted infusions of flowers in water. They are taken orally a few drops at a time, several times a day. Each flower essence embodies the harmonious vibrational pattern of the particular flower used, and thus resonates and attunes specific energy patterns within human beings.

The essences stimulate an enhanced awareness and ability to transform limiting attitudes, emotions and behavior into more creative and health-affirming ways of living. As such, flower essences harmonize well with other health and growth modalities. They can be effectively integrated into an overall program of health enhancement, including exercise, nourishing diet, stress reduction/relaxation, balanced life style, and appropriate medical care when needed.

Flower essences serve as catalysts to awaken the natural life force and spiritual consciousness within us. Through a dynamic interaction with the essential, life-affirming energies of Nature, we stimulate our own creative powers in a way that harmonizes with the entire planet.

Steve Koke

Sun-infusion of Sweet Pea flowers in water.

From the Editor:

EARTH-SPIRIT

Michael Pinter

Richard Katz

The Flower Essence Society has given birth to EARTH-SPIRIT, a vision of human harmony with the spiritual source of all life expressing itself on earth, a vision which provides the larger context for our work with flower essences. One form this vision is taking is the creation of a non-profit educational and research organization with which the Flower Essence Society will be associated. *(See the FES Members' Newsletters for updated information on specific legal and structural details.)*

We see flower essences as both a pathway to, and as a living symbol of our possible attunement with Earth and Spirit. By helping us transmute specific emotional blockages, negative attitudes, misperceptions and false identifications, they clear the way to our experience of the spiritual ground of being which is our link to all expressions of life with which we share this planet.

As more and more people feel the upheaval of planetary transformation, it is likely that increasing numbers will reach for flower essences for assistance. This would certainly be a hopeful development. Yet, we should be watchful for the temptation to fit the essences into a cultural bias which overemphasizes objects and techniques. The essences are not simply another addition to our array of ("new age") tools for coping with life in the world. They are a gift of the spiritual force which animates life, and they are mirrors of the life energies and capacities which are inherent within our souls. In preparing and using flower essences, our deeper lesson is to be receptive to the life force which they embody, and to re-awaken that life energy flowing within our own being.

If flower essences do become popular items in the new age/holistic health marketplace, we will need to remind ourselves of the source from which they spring, and to which they are ultimately leading us. It is the purpose of Earth-Spirit to give emphasis to this basic spiritual and philosophical dimension of flower essences.

These same deeper meanings were expressed in Dr. Bach's life and work a half-century ago, for it was out of his profound sensitivity to the spiritual basis of all life that the Bach Flower Essences were developed. Yet, even more significant than his preparation of these 38 marvelous remedies, was his comprehension of the inner language of Nature as expressed through the flowers, and his translation of the flowers' messages into the language of human experience. In the years since Dr. Bach's passing, however, the tendency has been to regard his achievement as an isolated miracle of human history, somehow inaccessible to others. We are now beginning to realize that the extraordinary attunement that Dr. Bach demonstrated is a long-neglected and undeveloped capacity of the human soul.

A comparable level of attunement with Earth and Spirit was demonstrated in the experience of the Findhorn Garden in northern Scotland in the 1960's. This was an experiment in the conscious co-operation of human beings with the consciousness which animates plant life. The messages which came through such people as Dorothy Maclean and R. Oglivie Crombie (Roc) not only instructed the gardeners how to grow more vibrant flowers and vegetables in that sub-arctic climate, but expressed the urgings of the natural world for human cooperation in restoring the balance of life on earth. (See our book review section in this issue.)

Our challenge is not to imitate Dr. Bach or the Findhorn gardeners, but to find our own form of communication with the source of life. Some of us will be able to directly tap into the language of subtle plant energies; others will find in art or music a link to the rhythms of Earth/Spirit. Each of us, however, can find some personal way of realizing and expressing our spiritual relation with the greater family of life.

For many, the realization is growing that the life-and-death crises that our world now faces are symptoms of the need for this renewed awareness of the interconnectedness of all life. The environmental and ecology movements began with the awareness that we must live with the consequences of our actions, that we cannot pollute the air and water, deplete material and energy resources and devastate natural beauty without destroying the quality of our lives. Now we are seeing that it is not just a matter of changing policies, but we must change our basic perceptions. Instead of feeling ourselves separate from a Nature we must "conquer," we must know ourselves to be participants in a planetary system of life (personified as the planetary being "Gaia"). The way out of ecological (and economic) crisis is not some new problem-solving plan to manipulate Nature. Rather, it is the creation of a new way of life, one that acknowledges our co-creative responsibility with the spiritual forces and energies with which we share this Earth. What is more, these forces and energies are willing and able to lend us considerable assistance in the job of creating this new awareness, as the examples of the flower essences and of the Findhorn garden have demonstrated.

"... our co-creative responsibility with the spiritual forces and life energies with which we share this Earth."

It may also be that only through such an awareness of "spiritual ecology," of our belonging to a planetary family of life, that we humans can overcome the tragic divisions that divert so much of our energy into destructive conflict. World peace and justice cannot be built on political power games; nor are idealistic sentiments by themselves sufficient to do the job. We need a practical understanding of our responsibilities as citizens of Earth, grounded in a deep realization of our brotherhood/sisterhood with all forms of life. The movements of the sixties for peace and justice, with all the good they did accomplish, had the tragic flaw of perpetuating much of the illusion of separation that is the cause of the problems they sought to overcome. Now, after a decade of spiritual deepening, a new political/spiritual synthesis is emerging, a movement whose actions spring from a deep sense of the unity of all life. (See "Planetary Resources.")

In re-awakening our sense of the sacredness of life, we have much to learn from the Native Americans and other peoples with a living tradition of harmony with the natural forces, of walking in balance with the Mother Earth. Yet we need not reject all the intellectual and technological accomplishments of our modern civilization. Earth-Spirit is not about a romantic "return to nature" in which we would try to escape our cultural identity. We intend to keep the best of our scientific and technical knowledge, and marry it to a primal awareness of our spiritual roots in the Earth. We can have computer networks and organic gardening, too.

It is important to see our present challenges in the context of the broad sweep of human evolution. In the book *Cosmic Memory* (Blauvet, N.Y.: Steinerbooks, 1976), Rudolf Steiner describes earlier human races which could tap directly into the life forces of plants and make use of their energy, even to the point of directing the course of plant species evolution. This deep resonance between human and plant (and animal) life was instinctive and intuitive. As humanity developed the rational faculties of the conscious mind, however, it began to lose its sense of connectedness with the rest of life. We have seen an acceleration of this process in recent history, until we have now reached a point of such imbalance that the contradictions of our present way of life prevent any further development without fundamental change.

At the same time that unbalanced technology is heading for this dead-end, the seeds of a new balance, a new synthesis, are being sown. The scientific investigations of the rational mind are leading us to the same realization of the interconnectedness of all life that stirs in our unconscious memory. New Physics speaks of the vibrational flux behind all reality, and measurements are made of the responses of plants to human emotions. Science and spirit converge.

Our challenge is to have the courage to move to the next level in the spiral of human evolution. Our developing experience of unitive awareness is not a regression to an unconscious past. Rather, it is an emergence into the light of consciousness, using the full spectrum of human faculties, and doing so with the conscious realization of our rootedness in Earth and Spirit.

The Earth-Spirit Vision

To express the vision of Earth-Spirit, we use not only the printed word, as in this journal, but also the various artistic media, which often seem to come closer to expressing the subtle energies and interrelationships which is our experience of deep attunement. This artistic direction is exemplified in the transformative art we feature in this journal, and in our upcoming project of joining with metaphysical

"EARTH MAN SPIRIT"

David Sherrod

harpist Joel Andrews to bring through music of the flowers. We encourage artists and musicians to use their talents to convey the message of harmony and wholeness to all who can see and hear it.

Another direction for the Earth-Spirit vision is the marriage of botanical science with spiritual awareness. We want to work with others in promoting gardens and plant sanctuaries where true appreciation of the plant world can be taught and demonstrated. This would include knowledge of plant structure and growth, historical and current plant uses, as well as the vibrational and spiritual dimensions of plant life. One of the areas we are now personally investigating is the study of Goethean and anthroposophical science relating to the spiritual significance of plant morphology and development.

Important to the fulfillment of Earth-Spirit's goals is the broadening and deepening of our educational efforts. We see the expansion of in-depth training programs for flower essence practitioners, coordinated with educational activities which promote an understanding of our responsibilities and opportunities for personal and planetary transformation. We see the education of children as a key element in this transformative work, and will support such efforts as Planetary Citizen's "Universal Children's Gardens" which demonstrate to children their familial relationship with the world of Nature.

In the area of research, we seek to bring together science and spirit by encouraging specific projects and programs which apply scientific discipline and methods to the exploration of flower essences and related phenomena, yet which retain a sensitivity to the spiritual dimension of life. As this is easier to articulate in principle than to translate into specific activities, we urge any of our readers with skills, interests or contacts related to such spiritual scientific research, to contact us. At this point our role is to be communicators and catalysts; we need your help to bring the Earth-Spirit vision into manifestation.

". . . we need collective action to alter the course of human society."

We also encourage the translation of Earth-Spirit ideals into action in the social and political realms. Transformation of consciousness is not an abstract process that takes place in isolation from social reality. Not only is individual change required, but we need collective action to alter the course of human society. Indeed, the most realistically "hopeful" prospect for global change of consciousness may be that the severity of the developing economic, ecological and political crises will wrench people free of their conditioned complacency, and propel them into a collective struggle for survival, out of which may emerge (we

pray!) a new realization of the profound interconnectedness of all life. We intend to do what we can to promote that realization, and suggest you contact some of the groups in our "Planetary Resources" listing, or find your own way to become a spiritual warrior for Mother Earth.

Each of us can join in this effort from the places and activities to which we are inwardly guided. We see the importance of land centers as examples of practical and spiritual understanding of our relationship with the Earth, and we hope to help create or become part of such a center as a base for our work. We also acknowledge the importance of people working within population centers, with their close access to the communications media and ability to help many people seeking spiritual guidance. From many streams of activity there is emerging a planetary network of individuals and groups, each working in their own way and within their own milieu, yet sharing a common vision and purpose in the healing of the planet.

Earth-Spirit will take its place as one of a number of focal points in this planetary "network of light." In this role, our work echoes the messages of new age organizations and communities throughout the world. What is unique about our gift, however, is that we bring the depth of experience of the flower essences to this planetary healing work, sharing the essences with our brother and sister groups, as we share the planetary perspective with our network of flower essence practitioners. We invite your support of this work in whatever form you can offer.

In this issue

With this fourth issue of our publication, we expand our *Flower Essence Quarterly* into an annual *Flower Essence Journal*. (Along with this change Flower Essence Society members now receive a bi-monthly newsletter.) Two major series of articles published in previous issues reach their conclusions in this issue: "Botany of the Bach Flowers" by Darrell Wright and "Exploring California Flower Essences" by Richard Katz. In other articles, we summarize some practitioners' clinical experiences with the FES essences, and discuss how astrological counselors are using Bach and FES essences in their practices. Other features represent some of our new Earth-Spirit directions. An excerpt from David Spangler's *Conversations with John* gives a unique spiritual perspective on the challenges of this decade. An interview with veterinarian Richard Pitcairn discusses the application of flower essences in animal health care, and probes the deeper philosophical issues involved in human relationships with animals. As a special artistic feature, we present the writing and mandalic art of John Tingley (our cover artist). Rounding out the issue are book reviews which present the story of plant-human communications and its lessons for the human community, as well as an excerpt from Suzanne Garden's upcoming book which gives a fresh look at the qualities of the Bach Flower Essences. The section of case studies announced in our last issue is now included as a regular feature of the FES Members' Newsletter, so it does not appear here. Also, Denise Diamond's (formerly Denni McCarthy) *Living with the Flowers* is being made available as a book, so it is not continued in this issue.

For latest information in flower essence research, case studies, practitioner reports, class and other announcements, *Journal* readers are encouraged to join the Flower Essence Society and receive the Members' Newsletter.

☙❧

PLANETARY RESOURCES

Bear Tribe Medicine Society
Sun Bear and Wabun
P.O. Box 9167, Spokane, WA 99209, USA

Native American teachings on healing and Earth awareness are presented in a cross-cultural and planetary perspective. They publish *Many Smokes* magazine and conduct Medicine Wheel Gatherings.

Holyearth Foundation
Danaan Parry and Lila Forest
Box 873, Monte Rio, CA 95462, USA

Right livelihood and responsibility for the Earth are emphasized through the Earth Steward program and "To Change Our World" workshops. They publish a calendar diary, *The Essene Book of Days,* and put out a quarterly newsletter.

Findhorn Foundation
François Duquesne, focalizer
The Park, Forres, IV 36 OTZ, Scotland

This pioneering international spiritual community was famous in the sixties for attunement with plant energies, and is now a center for planetary networking of spiritual groups, workshops and conferences, and community living. They publish and distribute many excellent books, and put out a bi-monthly magazine *One Earth.*

Lorian Association
P.O. Box 147, Middleton, WI 53562, USA

Founded by David Spangler and others from the Findhorn community, Lorian is a spiritually oriented educational association serving planetary culture with educational and creative arts programs for the public. They publish books on planetary themes and produce cassette tapes of new age songs by the New Troubadours.

New World Alliance
733 15th St. N.W., 180;11131, Washington, DC 20005, USA

NWA applies new age ideals to practical social and political concerns in a way that transcends the old divisions of left and right, and of spiritual and material. They have published a *Transformational Platform.* Membership includes a subscription to *Renewal,* an informative "transformational" newsletter edited by Mark Satin, author of *New Age Politics: Healing Self and Society.* (*Renewal,* P.O. Box 43241, Washington, D.C. 20010, USA.)

P.E.A.C.E. Network
Catherine Haydock
Truth Research Foundation
P.O. Box 77758, Stockton, CA 95207, USA

P.E.A.C.E. Network (Power to Energize Acceptance, Cooperation and Equality) is a network of individuals who, by sharing a personal commitment to peace, are co-creating a New World Spirit through conscious linking.

Planetary Citizens
Donald and Martha Keys, co-directors
777 United Nations Plaza, New York, NY 10017, USA

PC promotes world peace and understanding with a unique blend of spiritual awareness, psychological insight and political savvy. They issue Planetary Passports, sponsor the Universal Children's Gardens and publish a semi-annual magazine *Planet Earth,* and a newspaper *The Initiator.* Their focus for 1982–3 is the Planetary Initiative for the World We Choose, which begins with local citizens' caucuses on world issues, and culminates with a planetary conference of representatives and "wise persons" to chart a new course for human society.

These are groups with which we have recently been in contact. This is not intended as a comprehensive list. Reader suggestions are welcomed.—Ed.

A VISION FOR THE EIGHTIES

from *Conversations with John,* edited by David Spangler

****

We are a people fascinated with the future, toward which we seem to be hurtling at dizzying speed. Filled with images of planetary destruction and rebirth, we are at once expectant and appalled. In such a state we become hungry for any words of guidance we can find, whether or not they truly nourish our understanding. This is especially true of messages received psychically from sources beyond the physical plane. While these communications can some-times offer us valuable perspective, too often their effect is to turn us away from our INNER responsibility to trans-form the world. Instead, we can become obsessed with predictions of external events (Will California really fall into the ocean?), and how we might be saved from harm.

In this climate it is refreshing indeed to discover David Spangler's clear, conscious transmission of the wisdom and compassion of John. As a spiritual being viewing our world from another realm, John reminds us that we who are embodied on Earth are also spiritual beings, and our responsibility is to transform our lives here to express that universal Spirit on Earth.

The apocalyptic dangers of our time—nuclear war, eco-logical catastrophe, cataclysmic Earth changes—are the physical manifestations of our culture's inner devasta-tion—the cruel, uncaring way we treat ourselves, each other, and all life on this planet. There is nowhere we can (or should) go to escape from this apocalypse; we must be spiritual warriors who are ready to plunge into the heart of darkness and transform it with our light and love. To meet this challenge we need physical stamina and skills, but we need also spiritual strength and wisdom. We need our physical tools for growing food and building shelter, but we need also our spiritual tools (of which flower essences are an example) for transforming consciousness and opening hearts. Spiritual survival depends fundamentally on our awareness of universal Spirit, and our practical ability to give personal expression of that awareness in our daily lives. Then, wherever we may be, and whatever may happen, we can find security in our ability to break through the false barriers of separation and reach out to others in loving service. This truly is a vision for our times.
—Ed.

****

To us, the issue here is not prophecy, but the power of making skilled and appropriate responses to individual and world events through proper attunement. Many times in history, individuals, perceiving a threat coming from a certain direction, prepare themselves accordingly, only to discover to their regret that another threat comes from an unsuspected direction. Having invested their attention, energy and preparations in one direction, they are unpre-pared to meet this new threat, which may not be intrin-sically as powerful as the first one, but becomes more dangerous by virtue of being unsuspected. . . .

". . . three-quarters or more of your world experiences hopelessness . . ."

The vulnerability of the United States and of the world as a whole lies in its psychological depression, vibrating to a vision of confrontation and hopelessness. You, who live in the wealthy countries, perceive the possibility of con-frontation in the future, such as with the Soviet Union. To us this is a side-issue, diverting attention from more funda-mental planetary problems. A key area of challenge for us is that three-quarters or more of your world experiences hopelessness and is engaged in a struggle of the human spirit to surmount great physical and psychological difficul-ties. These people are focused on simple survival, and their struggle permeates the unconscious of your whole race with a similar vibration. In this way, no matter where you live, the vibrations of struggle permeate your environ-ment. This is not a joyous or confident struggle, but one filled with hopelessness, seeing little beyond the certain arrival of death. This vibration fills your world with an inertia of fatalism and depression, which impinges upon and affects even those of you who are not directly con-fronted with the problem of physical survival. It influences how you will see your problems and the inspiration and confidence with which you can meet them.

As long as this pervading energy of hopelessness is there, there is a vulnerability to images of destruction and an inability to transmute them adequately. Fear of both a definite and a vague nature moves through the hearts and minds of your people, challenging your powers of creativ-ity and erecting a fog or veil through which we workers in the realm of spirit must operate and which can diminish our efforts on your behalf. The crucial planetary challenge will not be resolved until those members of humanity who are free from the daily struggle to survive, who have been blessed with abundance, and who, therefore, can place themselves into attunement with wider spheres of creativity and vision, direct their energies to assist those who have no hope by giving them hope and substantive help.

On our level, we naturally do not identify life with a physical body; consequently, to us, the loss of your physical form is not a tragedy in the way that it might be for you. The deaths of millions of people is not in itself a tragedy for us, for it simply means their birth into our domains. What is a tragedy, however, is the loss of even one person because either lines of separation have been drawn, which shut out love, sharing, and human communion, or fear, neglect, and hostility have been allowed to determine your actions. When multiplied by thousands and millions of persons, it becomes a great planetary catastrophe which pollutes the inner, creative environment with vibrations of anger and fear, hopelessness and depression. All of you, and all of us, suffer from this. The lack of certain inner qualities, such as love and caring which transcend time and space, reverberate through the human species in ways that simple outer actions cannot. You do not face the ghosts of those who have died; but you do face the ghosts of neglected and forsworn opportunities to affirm your human wholeness and unity. You face the ghosts of those actions and, most importantly, those attitudes that foster fragmentation and separation. . . .

You place great importance upon spiritual prophecies of earth changes or of conflicts which could result in great destruction and loss of life. To us, such events are relatively unimportant. Where you look at external events for images of death and destruction, we look at the inner environment of humanity and see the same. We see ways in which consciousness chooses to fragment itself within itself, and from others, in the interest of what it calls its own well-being and protection. We see how it absolves itself from caring for the other members of its own wholeness, and we see where this creates death-in-life. We see the ground of love being split asunder along fault lines of ignorance and fear, and we see lives being swallowed up into the resulting chasms of despair. We see wars of inner intent being waged, which do not kill people outwardly, but which kill their spirits and isolate them from their higher principles of being, joy, hope and creativity. We see them becoming psychological, emotional casualties.

We see you creating your own Armageddons daily. This, to us, is the evil of your world. There is a tendency within human beings to look towards powerful external forces for explanation, to see a satanic being to whom they can attribute the sources of evil, or to see in those who have power and influence in your world evidences of con-

spiracies of control and manipulation. To us, the sources of evil lie in each human heart and mind and they are called fear and inertia. The resultant attitudes cause you to express your personal and collective energies against each other rather than to seek to understand and communicate with each other. It is true that there are certain beings and places where this evil accumulates, and that there are intelligences, largely drawn from within humanity itself, who find in suffering an energy which they can use as a form of vitality that allows them to maintain an illusion of separation from and power over the greater whole. However, such separation cannot last, for balance is always being restored. Yet these forces could not perpetuate the Armageddons in which you live if you did not choose daily the roots of Armageddon—the attitudes and actions by which you order your lives.

"We see the ground of love being split asunder along fault lines of ignorance and fear . . ."

A great deal of glamor, speculation, drama, fear and titillation surrounds the interest that many people have in predictions of the future, particularly those that foretell of wars or of destruction. Often, in the back of their minds is the sense that these phenomena will happen "out there" and not to them, or else they wish to know what might happen so that they can find a place of safety. Yet I can say with confidence that there is no place that anyone can go in the world where he or she can be safe. The dangers and challenges are not physical. Where can you go to be free from the inner cry of humanity for help and solace? Where can you go that the psychic toxins of fear and hopelessness cannot reach you? Why would you wish to be isolated from them, in any event? In truth, there is only one place, and that is alignment with God and Spirit. This alignment is a force that does not try to avoid these poisons of the psyche but embraces them, heals them, and reaches out to care and share of itself. It is an alignment with the presence of Peace, born of each person's efforts to give of himself or herself in service to each other and to the world. . . .

What we . . . offer you is an energy and a vision. We see you as being caught in currents of hopelessness and being mesmerized by danger. We would not lessen your perception of or alertness to what you must do to better your world. We would increase your perception of your inner security, protection and wholeness. We would increase hopefulness, for unless you can overcome your inertia and fear, you have no hope. Unless you can find the inner strength and joy, the stamina and boundless energy to challenge and go beyond your perceived limits, then you risk your worst dreams coming to pass.

The decade that is ahead will challenge you as human beings on all fronts of your lives: physically, emotionally, mentally, spiritually, economically, socially, politically. Yet, in the midst of this, there will be an increasing number of people who will be essentially untouched, who will be sources of protection, security, and new vision, whose energy will go into exploring and creating alternatives. These people will be those who are vessels of our spirit, and of their own high spirit, saying that there is hope and that the future can be recreated in the image of the divine. The responsibility and challenge which disciples of light face is how to be aligned with this creative effort, how to communicate it, extend it, share it, and demonstrate it. It is your responsibility as human beings to work out for yourselves how to do this. The new age is the age of your spiritual maturity when you do not need us to point out the obvious nor to direct you in living up to your highest; it is an age when we can each offer each other the best of our perspectives and energies and we can co-create together.

"Ultimately, all human beings are allies in the single battle against fear and inertia."

In moving through the times ahead, becoming emotionally overwrought at the sins and ills of the world, becoming sympathetic or guilt-ridden about the damage that humans do to each other and to the world will not help you. These are responses of glamor usually born of your attempts to avoid your own pain and transformative energies by focusing on lesser emotions. What is needed is precise, appropriate, skillful, wise, loving and serene action, thought, and attunement, filled with power and open to the true pain of your time and to the potentials of healing that pain. The universal spirit, which I call the Christ, pours its limitless spirit upon all peoples, upon the land, and upon your world as a whole. It is up to you to carry that spirit outward into action, thought, and relationship to the best of your abilities. If in so doing you find yourself entering into conflict or confrontation with people, institutions, or forces outside yourself, then do so without conflict in your own heart and mind. Do so without seeing these people as being less than brothers and sisters, but part of your wholeness. Do so without losing your vision of the ultimate harmony of all things. If you can grapple with your common foes, of fear and inertia—even when it takes the form of another person—if you can do so without fearing the other and without seeking to cast the other out, then your confrontations will become mutual grapplings with a common enemy, and you will then discover means of conflict resolution that draw on the essential

Niki Broyles

unities you share with others. Ultimately, all human beings are allies in the single battle against fear and inertia. Let this idea guide you in whatever conflicts you may enter and throughout the challenges and opportunities of this decade.

As you meet the challenges throughout the years ahead and rejoice in the opportunities and unfoldments that will also come, remember the presence of spirit. We are with you as co-creators. We look to the spirit within you with respect, with love, and with our own rejoicing, for we know that it will be this spirit that will transform your world. Do not doubt it, but be of good cheer. The future can be nothing but the shadow of your present. Look to the moments of your lives right now, for here lives that spirit and that power which you seek. May the blessings of that spirit enrich your lives and your vision, and be the daily unfoldment of the worlds we share.

Reprinted, with permission, from Conversations with John, *edited by David Spangler (Lorian Press, 1980).* © *1980 by the Lorian Association. For copies send $3.00 ppd. to Lorian Association, P.O. Box 147, Middletown, WI 53562, USA.*

Book Reviews

We know the flower essences as messengers of inner harmony and light, with songs of balance which resonate with what is deepest and most essential within us. As we learn the flowers' healing music, we also open our ears to the greater symphony of life of which they are a part. Their melodies beckon us to a joyful reunion with Nature, through the reconciliation with our own inner nature. Once we know this inner harmony, we can link with others to create such an attunement within the human community. Those of us who hunger for the experience of life's unity will find inspirational food in these three books.

❦

The Findhorn Garden: Pioneering a New Vision of Man and Nature in Cooperation, by the Findhorn Community. (New York: Harper and Row, 1975), 180 pages.

> One radiant energy pervades and gives rise to all life. While it may speak to us through plants, nature spirits or the human beings with whom we share life on this planet, all are reflections of the deeper reality behind and within them.
>
> *The Findhorn Garden,* page i

The Findhorn Garden is a well-woven tapestry of narrative, philosophy, spiritual channeling and visual imagery (superb photography!), which presents Findhorn's pioneering experience of cooperation with Nature. The outline of the story is familiar to many of us. Three people receive spiritual guidance to settle in a desolate trailer park in the wild north of Scotland. Their inner receptivity opens the way to contact with the plant "devas"—the "shining ones" or angelic beings who guide the formative forces of plant growth. The guidance ranges from specific instructions for planting vegetables to philosophical discussions of human relationships with Nature and Spirit. With this spiritual assistance, a garden is established which flourishes spectacularly, defying all known horticultural principles. It becomes a living demonstration of the potential co-creative relationship of humanity and Nature, and Findhorn becomes a center for those seeking to experience the unity of life.

What may be less well known about the Findhorn experience, but which seems of equal importance, is that within the principle of unity there is much room for diverse individuality. Each of the participants in the Findhorn saga—Peter Caddy, Eileen Caddy, Dorothy Maclean, Roc, David Spangler and other Findhorn community members—has his/her own story to tell. Each is an individual with his/her own personality and will, and each has consciously chosen to act in accordance with spiritual guidance in a way uniquely appropriate to his/her own soul path.

The various devas and angelic beings who are also a part of the Findhorn experience have their own individuality. They are not gods to be worshipped, for there is only one Source, one transcendent divine principle. Rather, the devas are brother/sister beings who challenge us to live up to our co-responsibility for life on this planet.

❦

To Hear the Angels Sing: An Odyssey of Co-Creation with the Devic Kingdom, by Dorothy Maclean. (Elgin, IL: Lorian Press, 1980), 217 pages. Also published by Findhorn Publications.

> You can render the greatest of services by recognising us and bringing our reality to human consciousness. It is fact that we are many, yet speak with one clear voice; it is fact that we are the overlighting intelligence of each species, not the spirits of individual trees; it is fact that we are vitally concerned with the Earth as a whole. Because we see mankind interfering detrimentally with the unit which you call this planet, we would communicate with him to make him more aware of divine law. The devas have been part of human growth in the distant past; we are part of that growth now, growth which has led him to self-consciousness and now to god-consciousness. Recognise our role, recognise God's life in all. Mankind as a whole does not recognise us. You can strongly emphasize that Nature is not a blind force, that it is conscious and has inner vehicles. Then man, as he comes to truth, will recognise us with his higher mind in spite of his intellect, and then he will fulfill God's purposes. We are grateful for any spreading of this truth.
>
> The Tree Devas

To Hear the Angels Sing, p. 135, copyright 1980 by Dorothy Maclean.

We know Dorothy Maclean as the messenger of the Findhorn devas, who call upon humankind to help restore the planetary balance of life. It is a timely message, and *To Hear the Angels Sing* is eloquent in its presentation. Yet Dorothy Maclean's story, with all its universal implications, is also a very personal history. We follow her life from childhood, through marriage and divorce, the Findhorn garden experience, and her time in northern California applying the messages of the devas to her own inner awareness and growth. She appears to us as someone not so unlike ourselves, but as one who has had the courage to follow the guidance she heard within, and to open herself to a wider world of possibilities than most of us allow.

Some readers may look to a story of contact with the angelic realms to feed their hunger for fascination and glamour. Instead, they will find this book to be an engaging story of a woman's spiritual evolvement. The devas offer us an inspiring reminder of attunement with divine purpose. But it is our uniquely human challenge to apply that divine light to the world of physical embodiment, to wrestle with free will and make the difficult choices and deep changes needed to bring our individual and collective lives into alignment with the divine order.

Niki Broyles

Faces of Findhorn: Images of a Planetary Family, by the Findhorn Community. (New York: Harper and Row, 1980), 177 pages.

Ultimately, Findhorn is a place of communication, from which communion and community may develop. This is what a planetary culture is, too; the matrix from which a true planetary communion and community may emerge, not simply a world government or economy. In our time we are learning to stop telling our tales so urgently and insistently and to listen to the world again. It is Findhorn's role to be a microcosm of this exchange; a place of listening, of sharing, of communication and community.

David Spangler, *Faces of Findhorn,* p. 3.

Findhorn's faces are its blossoms today, as the lessons learned in the garden are applied to the cultivation of human spirit and community. *Faces of Findhorn* is a moving depiction of that on-going process, replete with verbal and photographic portraits of individual and group experiences. Having contacted the essential spiritual core of life, the task now is to put that awareness to work in the daily life of a community of individuals. Such chapters as "Relationship and Community," "Politics and Synergy," "Manifestation, Finance, and Right Livelihood," show that the work has begun in earnest.

The Findhorn story is not just an account of 300 particular people living in a special place on the planet. It is a story that each of us can apply to our own lives and communities, as we seek to make the vision of a planetary family a living reality.—R. K.

"... for any nature lovers who feel specifically drawn to conscious communion with the devas of the plant world, here are some angles that I have found helpful. Again, this communion starts from the highest level of our being, and the more divine we know it to be, the better. If I am free from worry, it is easiest for me to feel harmonious when I am outdoors, where I quickly reach a state of diffused delight and happiness. This state needs to be focused on the essence of the particular plant. The season of flowering, of the fullest expression of the plant, gives the most clues to its essence through its colour, shape and scent, and the uniqueness of leaf and stem. In winter the energy is withdrawn. If I couldn't get the feel of its essence, I would live with the plant for a while, even picking a flower to keep in my room. Any particular meaning that the plant had for me, or any personal knowledge of it, created a link. Straining for contact only built barriers, whereas Love and appreciation build togetherness . . ."

Dorothy Maclean, *To Hear the Angels Sing,* pp. 123–124.

MANDALIC ART

by John Tingley

John Tingley

We extend our deepest thanks to John Tingley for his fine work on the front and back of our journal and for the writings and mandalic drawings (the originals are in color) which are reproduced on these pages.

John is a professional architect and designer as well as a writer, artist and healer. Of particular note are the many mandalas he has channeled for individuals. He prefers to see such drawings as evolutionary tools by which each person can see an important and unique quality of his/her own (realized or unrealized) in a visible form, thus aiding in outwardly manifesting such energy in daily life. John feels that, "By representing such inner forces in graphic or third-dimensional form, one's understanding and feeling for life is expanded."

Just as flower essences represent new levels of healing through vibrational resonance, so John's art evokes this same principle in its form and emanation. Such work as this suggests new possibilities for art that can capture and integrate the actual experience of this emerging dimension of awareness. We have been touched by the extraordinary gift which John offers and we hope that you will be, too.
—Ed.

To me there are not mysteries, only beauties. The beauty of things together and the beauty that things can come together beyond the seeming boundaries of time and difference of form. To me the sun caresses a tree with as much passion as two lovers in a warm embrace. And so all things in existence strive to defy the boundaries of their bodies and in communion on some plane, prove the unity of all.

From each to each, the chain of existence is formed to pass love on above and below. The message of love permeates all. Anything given freely of itself gives in love and of love. The flower's message of love, disguised as beauty, color and scent, is taken by you and carried to other heights of expression. It becomes a gift for a loved one, decoration for a room, a scent or an essence. It moves ever outward in expanding waves, its qualities touching, reaching and embracing until it returns again to its seed source. And so we, like a single flower, are on a journey to expand and touch all existence. Finally, we return to ourselves and know all that we are.

I have been a bursting sun, a drop of falling rain, a flower, and a tree . . . Now I am an artist, a pen and a piece of paper; and the words which you now read, to be carried with you, through you, and transmitted by you until we meet again.

When I first beheld a blackberry flower, I was moved by the purity of its whiteness and the beauty of its simplicity. It seemed to create its own universe with petals curving up in a cuplike form to create space and the inside exploding like a starry night. Its image was one of a self-contained entity, the bush also radiated a sense of peace and balance.

At that time I felt that I had received no message of insight from the flowers, but as I write now after having taken the essence for two months and having finished and studied the drawing, I realized that its sense of completeness was its message. This message relates directly to the blackberry's inner qualities of "conscious manifestation and the creative power of thought."

As I viewed the drawing, I was continually surprised by its feeling of balance. I have done designs that are perfectly symmetrical yet radiate far more kinetic energy. I wondered why this drawing, which is asymmetrical and contains numerous spinning motifs, would feel completely balanced. I believe it is again the message of the plant coming through; peace and self-containment in motion.

William Shakespeare, a truly creative being, said of his own work, "I have never thought how it would be received, but that I should give it." All creative thought comes from this sense of completeness. A creative thought emerges only to be manifested and expressed. The "what" is of all importance, the "how" will be found in action, but the only "why" that matters is that it feels to be expressed. How it is received is up to the audience alone.

So at least part of the "what" of the blackberry flower is seen and felt as balance and completeness (which is the absence of fear and limitation). The "how" is through color, form and scent, its distilled essence, and here through words and art. The 'why' is to be experienced uniquely by each of us and expressed as a deepened understanding radiating out to all we touch.

Blackberry

Carnation

Waves of light, pulsating rippling through space. From each atom these pulses of light emanate, animating all matter. Thus all life is vibration experienced as light, love, color and sound. Nothing is static, all moves ever onward and upward in spiraling waves of light. To symbolically represent these vibrations is the intent of my art.

These drawings are an attempt to use art to transmit the feeling and inner knowledge that flowers and their essences can make themselves felt and known on many levels. The drawings can be called mandalas as they are circular and radiating in nature but I prefer to see them as tools. They are meant, not so much to be a thing of beauty in themselves, but to be, like the flower essences, a catalyst to a deeper understanding of existence. Its worth is not as an object, but what feeling it awakens in you. And if it has stirred in some way, your heart, it has pierced a veil to allow deeper understanding to flow forth; to experience the feeling that all existence is connected in the web of life and that we can communicate and touch each other beyond the seeming boundaries of form and mind.

Celestial

ASTROLOGY AND FLOWER ESSENCES:
An Overview

by Richard Lamm

However much astrology may be assailed by scientific skeptics, and however much it is degraded by mass-media hype, astrology is, at its best, a highly-developed system of transpersonal psychology and counseling. As with flower essences, the language of this "transformational" astrology is one of self-understanding and self-actualization, where blockages are seen as invitations to creative change, and life purpose as the unfoldment of an individual expression of universal Spirit. Since both astrology and flower essences work with harmonizing the patterns of the personality with our higher potential, the question naturally arises as to whether there are useful correspondences between the two systems.

Our examination of this issue begins with this article by experienced astrologer Richard Lamm, in which he advises us to avoid the temptation of formulating a rigid system linking astrology with flower essences. Instead, we should work with each individual as a unique experience, drawing upon the tools of astrology and flower essences as appropriate, but not limiting our attunement with pre-set formulae. —Ed.

In the practice of astro-psychological counseling the client often asks the question, "What can I do to work out the problem which you've just described and which I recognize in myself?" or, "Yes, I recognize this talent in me, but how do I liberate or develop it?" Many counselors will recommend a technique, meditation, affirmation or book which will aid the client in self-transformation, self-actualization and self-healing; or they may refer the client to a therapist or group with which they are familiar, which may be able to help the individual to help him/herself.

One day during a horoscope consultation, while discussing some psychological problems with a client, I realized that I was using Bach Flower Essence key words in the description of the problems. I wrote on a note pad the Bach essence which corresponded to that psychological state. The client was open to trying the essences and I explained how they worked and how to use them. After a period of five weeks I received a very positive report from the client, who showed very good progress in the self-healing process. Since that time the Bach Flower Essences

have been a major tool in my work, because they fulfill the needs of both client and counselor. For the client they answer the question, "What can I do?" For the counselor they are a therapy whose language is similar to astro-psychology. Once one is familiar with the interpretive language of flower essences, correlations with astrology are natural.

It is therefore unnecessary to formulate a rigid theoretical system linking astrological signs, planetary sign and house placement, and aspects between planets with flower essences. This would become a limitation since we are using the horoscope to read individuals and the intuitive "tuning-in" process would be inhibited by any arbitrary system linking astrology with the essences. For example, the Clematis state is usually present to some degree in most individuals who have Sun, Moon, or ascendent in the sign Pisces, or Neptune in the first house, or Neptune in negative (or sometimes positive) aspect to Sun, Moon or Mercury. This does not mean that all people with these positions or aspects will need Clematis; nor does it limit the Clematis state to the above astrological conditions. If during an astrological interpretation it appears that the client is indeed experiencing the Clematis state, then the flower may be recommended.

". . . bridging the gap between interpretation and counseling."

It may be that through practice we develop a loose personal system of associating the essences with specific astrological information; but a personally developed system, while it may work very well for one therapist, may be incomprehensible to another practitioner. Many personal systems when compared with one another are confusing or contradictory.

The aspects between planets in a horoscope are valuable in flower essence selection because they reveal how planetary energies are functioning together. For example the tensions, conflicts and blocks reflected by squares and oppositions, and the confusion and frustration reflected by the quincunx (150°), will suggest different essences. If the horoscope contains a square or opposition between natal Sun and Saturn, some of the possible Bach essences suggested could be Rock Water, Pine, Vine, Mustard, Elm or perhaps some combination of these. Possibly throughout the life of the individual most of the psychological states associated with these essences were experienced by him or her. Now it is necessary to ask which of these states is manifesting at the present time. Here, feedback from the client is important in determining the proper selection.

Unaspected planets reflect a lack of integration or a lack of confidence in expressing planetary energies and, depending on the planet and sign and house it occupies, the associated essence can be recommended. Also, it may occur that the skill and productivity associated with the sextile, or the understanding, harmony and growth associated with the trine in the horoscope, do not find a channel or outlet in an individual. For example, if we find the Moon trine or sextile (or conjunct) to Neptune in the horoscope, which would suggest strong intuition and the client has no faith in his or her intuition, then Cerato may be recommended to help liberate the intuition. The dialogue with the client provides the necessary information which guides the therapist in choosing the correct essence. If we discover jealousy (Holly) in the horoscope, how does the client handle this jealousy? Do they fear and fight against it and try to control it? (Cherry Plum) Do they repress it? (Rock Water) Or do they give up trying to do anything and become apathetic? (Wild Rose)

A horoscope is a complicated interworking of energies and depends so much on the balance of different and often opposite energies. A good horoscope interpretation depends on the ability of the astrologer to provide the individual with a balanced, overall view of themselves at the psychological and material levels. When a flower essence selection is correlated with a holistic astrological analysis, it provides an excellent method of bridging the gap between interpretation and counseling.

Niki Broyles

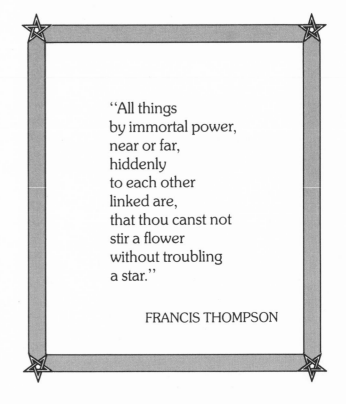

"All things
by immortal power,
near or far,
hiddenly
to each other
linked are,
that thou canst not
stir a flower
without troubling
a star."

FRANCIS THOMPSON

⚿ ⚿ ⚿ ⚿

STARFLOWERS:
Astrological Correlations to the Flower Essences
by Ellen Perchonock

Drawing upon her considerable experience as a counselor using flower essences and astrology, Ellen Perchonock describes how particular flower essences can be used with specific astrological signs and configurations. She cautions us, in agreement with Richard Lamm's preceding article, that these correlations are in no way definitive, and that each practitioner will need to use his or her own intuition and experience to develop connections between the two systems. The information which follows, therefore, is offered as an inspiration and preliminary guide to those seeking to explore the multi-dimensional relationship between astrology and flower essences.—Ed.

Introduction

In the self-healing process, we often work with both the immediate situation (stress, illness, life crisis) and the deeper, lifelong patterns underlying and leading up to that point. Consulting the astrological birth map of a person's energies and potential, as well as the transits and progressions indicating the current evolutionary stage of their life cycles, enables the counselor to develop a broader perspective of the whole person. Thus, the counseling session can be based on a view of the client which enhances the intuition and yet is not limited by subjective evaluation of the problem, or by the immediate energy patterns usually picked up by the pendulum.

In using this astrological evaluation to supplement the usual counseling with the Bach Flower Essences (and, more recently, the FES essences), several helpful correlations between certain flowers and specific factors in the birth chart have been observed over a period of years. (See Acknowledgements below.) These correlations were derived, for the most part, from experience, although many, of course, were originally inspired through meditation or direct intuitive knowledge.

The correlations can best be used as a guide to the selections of essences, to be further verified by intuition, the pendulum, etc.; they are by no means complete or definitive. In fact, since others have come up with different sets of correlations, practitioners seeking to use this selec-

tion aid would do well to learn each system (astrology, flower essences) fairly well, and then let their own intuition and experience derive the connections between the two systems. As we will see later, this can really only be done effectively by tuning in to the deepest level of meaning or essence of the energies that underlie the manifested behavior patterns. Another factor involved is the level at which the flowers are operating—the personality or the higher (inner, essential) self—in a particular individual. This may contribute to apparent discrepancies with other correlation schemes. Also, correlations derived from meditation may be different from those uncovered by intellectual analysis of the essences and planetary energies.

While some practitioners have had excellent results treating a client with just one or two flowers for a long period of time (several months), others find it appropriate to give two or three flowers for the immediate problem, and two or three for the more deeply-ingrained patterns with which the client wants to work consciously. It is in the latter case that the birth chart information can be of most help in guiding the practitioner to focus on specific sources of internal energy conflicts.

In my own practice, I try to deal first with the current situation as experienced by the client, which may include an explanation of any relevant astrological cycles (transits) corresponding to the manifestation of the problem at this time. This fosters a deeper insight into the cycles of growth and change in their lives. Next, I look at the birth chart and point out some salient features, noting areas of possible stress, along with suggestions for constructive use or transformation of the energies involved (depending on the person's level of self-awareness). After this, we attune through a brief meditation, at the end of which I let my hands move lightly through the person's aura, being guided to select several essence bottles from the box, usually five to ten. To these I add any intuitive choices and, if none of the flowers indicated by the astrological information has come up (which is rare), I will sometimes test a few of these. After confirmation of these selections by the pendulum, I discuss the qualities and effects of each flower, how to work with them as part of the healing process, and any other healing suggestions or practices that seem appropriate.

Signs and Planets

We will now consider some of the simpler and more obvious correlations with the twelve signs and their planetary rulers. Of necessity, the astrological information which follows is oversimplified. Also, these hypothetical general correlations should always be modified by taking into account the individual client's energies and situation.

Some of the flowers do not appear to have specific correlations; in particular, these are the ones having to do with the general energy flow of the etheric and other subtle bodies (**Olive** and **Hornbeam**), or with general crisis situations (**Rescue**), or chronic illness (**Gorse**). In the correlations which are listed below, each sign is listed with several common traits, each trait followed by the appropriate flower essence(s) and its transforming action for that trait.

Aries (Element: Fire; Ruler: Mars) For the headstrong, impulsive, speedy, impatient nature of the pioneering energy: **Impatiens,** to promote patience and reduce the irritability of having to wait for others; **Heather,** to see beyond the personal concerns and develop other-awareness. For the lack of self-discipline in indulging in experiences, drugs and other "addictions" which give "rushes:" perhaps **Morning Glory.**

Taurus (Earth, Venus) For the inability to let go of the material and emotional objects of security (possessions, people): **Chicory,** for helping release attachments. For the patient perseverance, struggling on with great strength: **Oak.** For the inflexible attitudes and stubbornness, leading to a lack of perceptiveness of self: **Chestnut Bud,** to allow the higher perception of one's actions to be seen and understood, to observe the patterns in which one is stuck.

Gemini (Air, Mercury) For the tendency of the energies to scatter in many different directions and projects: **Wild Oat,** to help focus these multi-talented energies into a few tasks at at time. For the tendency of the mind to conduct endless conversations with the self, with all possible ramifications and arguments, leading to nervous exhaustion: **White Chestnut,** to still the mind and help one achieve Zen-like empty mind. For the inability to hear the clear voice of intuition through all the mental static, turning instead to the myriad sources of external stimulation (people, media), creating even more confusion: **Cerato,** for balancing the logical mind with the intuition; also appropriate: **Madia, Shasta Daisy** and **Nasturtium.**

Cancer (Water, Moon) For holding on emotionally, clinging to past memories or people, having absorbed

them into the self as part of one's wholeness, for possessive love, for the maternal attachment to children: **Chicory,** for allowing one to let go and let love flow. For living in the past, nostalgia, regrets, etc.: **Honeysuckle,** to gently detach from the past and live fully and joyfully in the present.

Leo (Fire, Sun) For the tendency to dominate others, leadership based on ego-gratification: **Vine,** to allow the natural, inspirational leadership abilities to be expressed, while remaining flexible and sensitive to others, the energy flowing from the Higher Self and not the ego. For the tendency to over-do and exaggerate things, the dramatic flair: **Vervain,** to achieve the same accomplishments, but effortlessly, without strain, using the organizational talents.

Virgo (Earth, Mercury) For the tendency to be overly critical of others, seeking perfection around oneself, caught up in details: **Beech,** to increase tolerance for the faults of others, to allow oneself to feel whole and complete and perfect within self, using the power of analysis constructively for growth. For any feelings of impurity, feeling "dirty" or polluted by one's environment or situation: **Crab Apple,** to purify and cleanse the aura.

Libra (Air, Venus) For the indecision resulting from always being aware of the "other" viewpoint, of all sides of the situation: **Scleranthus,** to help one stay close to the center, to bring balance and to resolve extremes. For the hidden anguish behind the cheerful, sociable façade which one wishes above all to keep harmony among people, to please everyone, to keep the environment aesthetic: **Agrimony,** to allow a deep inner self-acceptance so that the pleasantness projected is drawing easily from inner joy and peace, not draining energy, nor compulsively hiding any negative feelings.

Scorpio (Water, Pluto) The essential Scorpio energy involves a spiritual urge to refine energy, eliminate dross, penetrate to the truth; giving up the ego through absorption into something greater than self, thus seeking emotional intimacy. For the negative expressions of the extremely intense, powerful desires, when turned against the self destructively, for smoldering resentments, bitterness, blaming others: **Willow,** to take full responsibility for what happens to one in the world, to allow the power to be expressed creatively and constructively. For the more actively, openly expressed negative emotions channeled towards others, jealousy, hatred and anger: **Holly,** to help transform these distorted energies into their true nature, great love and healing energy. For the guilt of self-blame that arises when people feel such intense negative states inside themselves: **Pine,** to allow one to take responsibility, but without guilt.

Niki Broyles

Sagittarius (Fire, Jupiter) For the over-expansiveness and tendency to exaggerate found in this sign of aspiring to the truth, to far horizons, both mentally and physically: **Vervain,** to quiet, center and relax the energies, and to contain their attempts to persuade and convert others to their own views. For the self-righteousness that may arise in moral, ethical and spiritual matters (since they are often wise and prophetic, and know it): **Beech,** for the tolerance to accept others' right to their own belief systems. For the scattering of the energies like lightning flashes in many directions: **Wild Oat,** to focus and concentrate the energies on the task at hand.

Capricorn (Earth, Saturn) This sign's essential energy is the crystallization of energy into the structure and limiting forms of the material plane, reflecting cosmic law and order, providing a channel for the manifestation of higher energies. For the tendency to be too hard on the self, for the inhibition of joyful self-expression, the "repression of the sublime," especially for moral and spiritual ideals: **Rock Water,** to give a greater acceptance and love of the self as inseparable from that spiritual–moral ideal, while still maintaining any necessary discipline. For deep depressions, gloom, being stuck in very dense energies, gripped by frustration, unable to free oneself: **Mustard,** literally to lighten up the energies, bringing the freedom of a more expanded perspective. For the bitterness, resentment and guilt that comes from feeling separate and isolated from others, frustrated in one's actions and expressions: **Willow,** to help one understand that outer difficulties are a reflection of the inner state, and that by feeling connected to others through love one has the power to manifest a more positive reality.

Aquarius (Air, Uranus) This is the sign of the New Age, combining the unique expression of the individual with a simultaneous awareness of the group energy—the tribe, the community, the planet; and the sign of the Universal Mind, higher intuition, representing all that is new, nonconformist, sudden, freaky, rebellious, transcending old limits. For the dignified aloofness and detachment that comes from the impersonal view of this sign, which sees everyone as equal and makes better contacts with people in general than with the individual: **Water Violet,** to help one be more open to the common everyday experience, to diminish the distance and coolness often misperceived as snobbery or pride, to be sympathetic. For the shock involved in Uranian experiences, inevitably sudden and throwing one off balance and out of center: **Star of Bethlehem** (a Rescue Remedy ingredient), to alleviate the effects of all shocks, mental, emotional and physical, to help re-center oneself, since *reaction* is all-important in Uranian events. For Uranus aspects or transits (see below) which create a very finely-tuned, "high-tension wire" nervous system, subject to spasms: calming and relaxing flowers such as **Impatiens, Vervain, Chamomile** and **Morning Glory.**

Pisces (Water, Neptune) This is the sign whose energy is least describable in concrete terms, being strongly connected with subtle planes representing collective feelings, archetypal energies and images; the person as a representative of the whole; and the ocean, dissolving away all forms and differences. For the psychic fears, fears of the unknown, absorbed like a "psychic sponge" from the other planes, people and the environment: **Aspen,** to allow the experience of faith and universal love to balance and release these fears. For the dreaminess, the tendency to escape into more beautiful idealistic and etheric realms: **Clematis,** for grounding on the earth-plane, so the subtler energies can be manifested in daily life. For the veil of illusion, delusion and "fog" that occurs on the physical plane when the higher aspects of Neptunian energy, meditative and creative activities, are neglected: **Shasta Daisy** and **California Poppy,** for clarity in spiritual knowledge, spiritual sight, etc. For the oversensitivity and "psychic-sponge" permeability of the aura: **Walnut, Pink Yarrow** and **Yarrow,** to protect and strengthen the aura against outside influences.

Using the Correlations

Aspects

In actual usage, one of the above correlations would probably be considered relevant if the Sun, Moon, Ascendant or a group of other planets were in a particular sign, *as well as* there being a major challenging aspect (see note below) to that Sun, Moon, etc. For example, the description for Sagittarius would not apply to someone who had a well-aspected Sun in Sagittarius and no other planets in Sagittarius. However, if that person had several planets in Scorpio, with squares in Pluto, then the essences listed for Scorpio/Pluto would be the most appropriate ones to try first. Another guideline involves (challenging) aspects to the *rulers* of the above sign. For example, **Impatiens** (an "Aries essence") would be appropriate for squares between Mars, the ruler of Aries, and certain other planets (Moon, Uranus, etc.).

The application of the correlations to the specific aspects of an individual horoscope is rather complex unless, as mentioned earlier, one is familiar with both systems and can rely on his/her intuition. Several very different energy patterns in a person may manifest in similar behavior or emotional states, which may need the same flower essence. For example, **Larch,** could be used for any of the following aspects: Sun square Saturn, Sun square or opposite Pluto, unaspected Sun and Sun square Moon; whereas **Centaury, Aspen** or **Clematis** could be used for the aspect Moon square Neptune. There are also considerations of the houses, elements, planets in certain signs, etc., which are too complex to present here, but follow in general from what has been said thus far. No simple listing of aspects, signs and flowers can give more than one facet of how this valuable counseling aid can work. The practitioner has to be creative in finding the essence for the difficulty of an individual at that particular time. (For further examples and explanations, please see the longer version of this article available from Ellen Perchonock, RFD Box 151A, Montague, MA 01351.)

Aspects

The aspects, or angles formed between the planets, reflect the degree and ease of integration of the whole dance of energies in a chart. Challenging (difficult, disharmonious) aspects—square (90°), opposition (180°)—create tensions and frustrations on an inner level, but also give the dynamic energy which spurs people to express themselves creatively, or begin a process of growth and change. Harmonious aspects—trine (120°), sextile (60°)—represent an easy combination of energies, innate talents which may not be developed, having been taken for granted, or used in an unaware way. Conjunctions, planets occupying roughly the same space (0°), in general the strongest aspect, are considered either harmonious or disharmonious depending on the planets involved.

Transits

As you learn to use all your energies productively and integrate them, you will begin to transcend your birth chart, and display fewer of the personality characteristics it indicates. The chart cannot show the level of your development in this lifetime, or how you will manifest your energy in detail. Rather, it is a map for your spiritual evolution, a guide for increasing your awareness of your Self-nature.

Transits, the relationships between planets in the sky at the moment and the planetary positions of your birth chart, indicate the timing of your cycles of unfoldment and growth. The transiting planets resonate with your basic energies, activating certain areas and presenting opportunities for change in them. The flower essences are extremely helpful in dealing with the effects of many transits, especially those of Saturn and Pluto, the most intense ones for most people.

These transits usually require the release of attachments to old forms, or transformations forced by crises, and channeling of one's energies into new directions. Thus, they involve a lot of resistance, for which **Chicory,** the "letting go" essence, can be very helpful. Two very helpful essences in general for these situations are **Sweet Chestnut,** for the feeling of floating alone in the void, in anguish, in that transition space between the familiar old and the unknown ahead, and to help bridge the gap and remain whole, not torn apart; and **Walnut,** for the strength to bear with the major life changes, sever the links tying you to the old and to what is outside you, and allowing your true inner self to emerge. For the heavy negative emotional patterns, often subconscious, that Pluto transits (and others) often cause to re-surface (even after you thought them gone or transformed), **Holly, Willow** and **Pine** are generally applicable. For Uranus and Neptune transits, several flowers mentioned above under Aquarius and Pisces may be helpful.

The return of Saturn to its natal position (between ages 28-30) marks the "coming of age," or maturity, in astrology. It requires the disidentification of the self with old habits, patterns and images derived from early family and cultural influences, and the unfolding of one's essential self, seeking to fulfill the life purpose. This may be a time of experiencing great frustration, depression, pain, resistance, problems or crises with authority and the father/family, etc. Many people seek out help at this time, and of course may be successfully helped with the flowers and other counseling without any awareness of the Saturn cycle. However, this detached perspective on a stage of the life cycle which is inevitable for all of us is usually a most welcome and enriching cycle for clients.

In addition to the flowers already mentioned, others that may be helpful at this time are: **Mustard,** for depression; **Sagebrush,** to help incorporate within one's inner being the true "order of the universe," thus easing the letting go of the old self, and the attachment to it as the only self; **Fuchsia,** to help relieve and transcend the frustrations and limitations; perhaps **Sunflower,** if the individual's Saturn transit requires dealing with the internalized male parental authority image; and for those undergoing great hardships: **Gorse, Scotch Broom** or **Penstemon.** (The Bach essences mentioned here have been found to be wonderful aids during these transits in the experience of many people; the newer FES essences are only suggestions, but have already begun to prove their value in such situations.)

Acknowledgements

The credit for developing these correlations belongs especially to the following individuals: Ionna Salajan, teacher of meditation and healing, including Bach Flowers; Richard Lamm, astrologer and group leader; Arya Kiekens, Bach Flower practitioner and astrologer; and Sita Cornelissen, who does aura balancing work with the flower essences; as well as many others in the Amsterdam community with whom I shared experiences, observations and discussions of these correlations.

Editor's Notes:

The following case is taken from the Flower Essence Society files and illustrates flower essence use during the Saturn transit:

A 29-year-old woman was experiencing her Saturn transit with Saturn retrograde. She felt stuck in a pattern of reaction based on her childhood experience with her very stern father. She found that she would alternately rebel and be overly aggressive, or try to eliminate her "ego" and become overly passive. **Sunflower** was indicated for a period of three months, during which time she began to develop a sense of her individuality based on her own identity and soul purpose, rather than as a reaction to her father's identity.

The following correlations are based on an article by Matthew Wood, a Flower Essence Society member, "An Astrological Herbal," pp. 206-231 of Llewellyn's 1982 Moon Sign Book *(St. Paul, MN: Llewellyn Publications, 1981):*

GEMINI:
Impatiens—for the quick Gemini who has a tendency to impatience and overstimulation
Elm—for "intellectual understanding of responsibility combined with susceptibility to outside ideas"
Dill—for "assimilation of experience"

CANCER:
Honeysuckle—for nostalgia

LEO:
Sunflower—"balanced expression of ego"
Chicory—to develop selfless love

VIRGO:
Willow—to accept guidance without resentment

LIBRA:
Red Clover—creating balance, overcoming hysteria

SCORPIO:
Holly—overcoming negative emotions with love
Iris—for feeling stuck in negative emotional patterns
Scarlet Monkeyflower (especially for Venus in Scorpio)—for fear of the power of the love desire

CAPRICORN:
Oak—to develop character through difficult trials
Penstemon—"strength through adversity" (from the alpine country, home of the Capricornian mountain goat)

AQUARIUS:
Star of Bethlehem—psychic balance in the face of great upheavals

PISCES:
Clematis—for unconsciousness, dreamy inattention

Editor's Afterword: *In addition to the above perspectives regarding the interrelationship of astrology and flower essences, we should also like to offer the thought that there is a virtually unexplored dimension of communion between stars and flowers.*

As we simultaneously move into deeper, more dynamic forms of communication with the plant world and also with planetary and stellar realms, we can begin to glimpse the interconnection of both worlds. Medieval herbalists/alchemists such as Paracelsus and Culpepper introduced significant work which sheds light on the ancient dictate, "as above, so below." Rudolph Steiner, a great seer and teacher in the early part of this century, further elucidated this path, teaching that as humankind enters into a deeper, more conscious understanding of Nature, so also the stellar worlds open. "Once the stars talked to man, now man talks to the stars," were the prophetic words spoken by Steiner to suggest this emerging relationship of humankind with the cosmos. We invite articles on this topic for publication in future issues of the journal.

Niki Broyles

"From the zodiac came the veritable secrets of God. The Star Angels are transmitters and flowers become symbols of their communication. The closer our communion with the Angels, the deeper will be our sense of the mysteries of the plant kingdom and the greater our realization of the spiritual ministry of the world of flowers."

Paracelsus

CLINICAL USE OF THE FES FLOWER ESSENCES

by Patricia Kaminski

Larry Miller

*Patricia
Kaminski*

*Since their introduction to the public in 1980, the new
FES flower essences have rapidly established themselves as significant tools in health and counseling
practices in many regions of the world. In its role as a
communications and research network for flower essences, the Flower Essence Society receives feedback
from practitioners throughout the United States and
Canada, and in such countries as England, the Netherlands, Germany, Australia, New Zealand, Switzerland
and many others. At the time of publication of this
article, the Flower Essence Society comprises about
1500 members, including nearly every state in the USA
and more than 15 countries throughout the world. The
members include interested laypersons, although a
large percentage of the membership includes active
practitioners who in turn reach many other persons.*

*Recently, FES co-director Patricia Kaminski conduct-
ed in-depth interviews with six practitioners who have
very active clinical practices. The interviews had the
goal of deepening our knowledge of how flower essences
—and particularly the new FES essences—are being
used. The following article is based on these interviews.
It provides important insights, not only on specific essences and techniques, but also on key attitudes and philosophical approaches to administering flower essences,
which all practitioners will want to consider. —Ed.*

Flower essences have the quality of being applicable
across a broad spectrum of health practices and life
styles. This attribute clearly emerged from our interviews with six flower essences practitioners, each of
whom evidenced a distinctly individual approach to their
practices and to the use of flower essences. Common
themes can be discerned in their experiences, but
it is the uniqueness of their approaches which is most
striking in what they share. It appears that the real key is
to find that form of work with the essences which best
suits the temperament and skills of a particular practitioner, especially as it harmonizes with that particular
person's path of service and spiritual evolvement. Since
flower essences themselves are teachers of the way of
inner attunement and individuation, it follows that the
practice of sharing the essences with others is governed
by these same themes.

The Practitioners

The six practitioners interviewed for this article represent a geographic and professional cross-section of
clinical use of flower essences. They include a progres-
sive medical doctor, a wholistic dentist, a naturopath, a
chiropractor, a polarity teacher and therapist, and a
spiritual healer. They also represent some (but certainly
not all) of the major centers of flower essence activity:
nothern and southern California, New York, Massachusetts and the Netherlands. All are members of the Flower
Essence Society.

Maryanne Jerome, M.D., is founder of the Mad
River Holistic Center in Arcata, California, located in the
northern California coastal Redwoods. Besides her training as a medical doctor, Dr. Jerome has professional
training in dance, music, massage and psychology. Elements of all of these skills are integrated in her health
practice, which focuses on counseling, massage, visualization and flower essences. She describes her massage
technique as "touch choreography," involving a combination of certain elements of dance, T'ai Chi Chuan and
massage. Although Dr. Jerome's practice does not

emphasize such conventional approaches to medicine as writing drug prescriptions, she believes that "there is not much of a dividing line between 'conventional' and 'alternative.' What works is what is important." Consequently, her work brings her into contact with mainstream doctors and hospitals, in addition to other creative, alternative activities.

Roy M. Smudde, D.D.S., is a dentist and wholistic health practitioner who helped to establish a wholistic center within the Cedars Sinai Medical Office Towers in Los Angeles, California. As a dentist he specializes in temporomandibular (TMJ) problems, relating tensions in the face and jaw to emotional and spiritual issues facing his patients. He works in cooperation with medical doctors, chiropractors, psychotherapists, nutritionists, masseuses and spiritual healers who are a part of the clinic, where flower essences are an important part of the total approach used at the Center.

Paul Andrews, N.D., has training in naturopathic medicine and herbology, and runs the Monterey Polarity Center along the central California coast. His practice incorporates botanical medicine (herbology), nutritional counseling, radiesthesia, polarity and manipulative therapy and flower essences. He specializes in pain control, using electro-acutherapy.

Michael Cindrich, D.C., is a chiropractor in New York City, whose work focuses on the sacro-occipital technique (S.O.T.), craniopathy, applied kinesiology, nutritional counseling and flower essences.

Suleman Aberman is director of the Polarity Center of Boston, Massachusetts, where he has his own holistic health practice. He is, as well, a teacher leading training programs for health practitioners in many different cities. His work has evolved from polarity energy balancing to include cranial-sacral balancing and more subtle work which he describes as a "process of unwinding the person through the nervous system, emotionally and spiritually, and at each stage helping them to experience the knot that was." Flower essences form an integral part of the practice and the training programs of the center.

Rebecca Spatola is a spiritual healer in Amsterdam, in the Netherlands, whose work grew out of her own healing crisis nine years ago, and her use of the Bach remedies to help bring her to new clarity. Since then she has studied many aspects of spiritual healing, especially opening channels of intuitive knowing. Such studies have included polarity, acupressure, body movement, color and visualization, music and sound, breath and psychic energy; as well as much direct healing and teaching work throughout her country where she introduces the Bach and FES essences to many persons.

Flower Essences within the Context of Health Practices

With each of these practitioners, we find that the essences are able to enhance the other aspects of their practices, and also that the various other approaches and methods are in turn able to facilitate a more effective use of the essences. For example, both Dr. Smudde and Dr. Cindrich work with structural tensions in the physical body which are related to mental and emotional tensions, and they find the flower essence integral to this process.

". . . when the essences are combined with other techniques, a kind of synergistic effect is noted . . ."

Dr. Smudde began with researching his own TMJ problem and came to the conclusion that there were four major aspects: 1) structural - joints, muscles, bones; 2) physiological and energy systems, including the acupuncture meridian system; 3) mental and emotional components; 4) spiritual factors involving a particular soul's evolution. In his practice, it became obvious to him that "The facial muscles carry many emotions. If you are uptight and stressed, you clench your teeth and squeeze your jaws, and you can see the . . . muscles just pulsating when people are tension-packed." He began using the Bach Rescue Remedy and other Bach remedies as adjuncts to his TMJ therapy to deal with these tensions, and later added the FES essences to work with the spiritual as well as the mental/emotional components of treatment. The essences became invaluable aids in allowing his patients to work consciously with the life lessons which were at the core of their healing process. At the same time, Dr. Smudde finds that it is usually necessary to work initially with the structure and vital energy of a patient before being able to effectively introduce the more subtle power of the flower essences. Thus, initial sessions often involve cranial osteopathy, homeopathy and acupuncture or acupressure before using the flower essences to address emotional, mental and spiritual issues.

Dr. Cindrich also finds in many cases that the structural work he does and the the flower essences support each other, "especially with an acute emotional problem that seems to be causing a psychosomatic response within the patient." By using flower essences as "supplements" to the chiropractic adjustments, he finds that the physical problems are more easily cleared up. It is not so much that there are specific correlations between emotions and particular chiropractic problems, but rather that "the patient's emotional patterns manifests sickness in a non-specific way," and then physical illness occurs at the weakest point.

Cindrich finds that some patients are very physically-oriented, and thus have a difficult time accepting the essences at first. However, many of these individuals become receptive to emotional work with the essences after they have been chiropractic patients. Others, he finds, come primarily for the flower essence work itself.

The other practitioners also combined flower essences with various health modalities they used. Dr. Andrews described the essences as a "catalyst" to enhance other methods in his practice. Dr. Jerome, Suleman Aberman, and Rebecca Spatola each use essences as part of an integrated approach with body work, counseling, visualization, music and other similar methods. Often it is not possible to specify the particular effect of the flower essences, and yet the practitioners agreed that the essences provided an important ingredient in their work that they would not want to do without. Most importantly, it seems clear that when the essences are combined with other techniques, a kind of synergistic effect is noted that is far more powerful than any single technique.

Selection Methods

There are four basic methods used by the practitioners in selecting essences for their clients: formal interview, applied kinesiology (muscle testing), radiesthesic analysis (involving a pendulum), and intuitive/psychic perceptions. Some practitioners reported a particular method which was preferred, while others combined methods or selected different methods according to the nature of their clients.

The interview is used by all the practitioners, to at least some extent. For Dr. Jerome and Dr. Andrews, it is the primary method of selection, although each one has some familiarity with radiesthesia, and allows intuition to play a role. After initial discussion has indicated a possible essence, Dr. Jerome usually has her patients look at the description of the essences in Phillip Chancellor's *Handbook of the Bach Flower Remedies,* or in the *Flower Essence Journal,* to see if the selection seems appropriate. Dr. Andrews feels that "part of their therapy is to discuss what is troubling them." He listens a great deal and takes notes as his patients talk, and he also observes voice tone and body language in assessing which essences are to be used.

Dr. Smudde, Dr. Cindrich and Suleman Aberman use radiesthesia as a major selection method along with the client interview. *(See Armstrong, issue #2, pages 7-9, for*

a fuller discussion of radiesthesia.) Dr. Cindrich makes use of an applied kinesiological technique using the pectoralis major clavicular muscle in a unilateral (one-arm) test, which he finds to be very keyed to the emotional state of a person. *(Please note adjoining box for a full description of this technique.)*

". . . selection is a process that involves both analytic and intuitive approaches . . ."

Aberman uses the pendulum with the lists of the essences to select the appropriate ones for his clients. As he is working with the pendulum, he feels "activity in the higher reaches of my consciousness." Usually he knows or has talked with the client so that the pendulum work becomes a kind of "data processing" in the intuitive mind. He maintains that there is no such thing as "objective healing," that there is no one right choice of essences. Rather, the flowers chosen will differ from one practitioner to another and are a manifestation of the relationship between the practitioner and client, and of the process of communication between them. New essences are chosen when the client appears ready for a new cycle, which may be two or three days, or as long as eight weeks, but is more commonly a period of two to three weeks.

Niki Broyles

Rebecca Spatola uses the intuitive faculties as her primary approach to selection of essences. Her method involves having the individual lay or sit quietly, to bring about a general feeling of centeredness and receptivity. She tunes into her own inner guidance and also to the level of soul attunement in her patient. She then sits and

Dr. Michael Cindrich tests for essences using an applied kinesiological technique with the pectoralis major clavicular muscle (a muscle strongly correlated with the emotional state of an individual). The technique is as follows: The individual lies supine on the back with both arms (initially) stretched toward the ceiling. The arms and wrists are rotated so that the backs of the hands can touch each other. First both arms are tested bilaterally by pulling them down towards the patient's feet at a 45° angle. Then a unilateral test is made by having the individual drop one of the arms, and testing the other. Dr. Cindrich finds this unilateral test to be very important for assessing emotional conditions, particularly where there is marked difference between this test and the bilateral test. When a significant difference is discovered, the essence bottle to be tested is placed in the individual's open hand, or a few drops of the essence are placed on the tongue, and the muscle is re-tested. If the essence is appropriate, there is a significant strengthening of the muscle.

waits until she feels inspired to speak to the client and she notes that the remedies "will often simply emerge into conscious thought." This naming of the essences is often accompanied by a sigh or other movement of energy which is usually felt simultaneously in both herself and her patient. In addition, Rebecca Spatola has developed sensitivity in her hands to the point where she is often able to pass her hands along a row of essence bottles and feel which ones are indicated. She confirms this selection by placing the bottle in the patient's energy field to ascertain whether or not there is a positive resonance. This same method of hand selection is often used quite successfully for plants and animals. In the case of children, she often has them make their own spontaneous selection, as their intuition is relatively pure and unblocked.

Intuition is used by other practitioners to varying degrees, often as an unspoken complement to the particular selection technique employed. From these examples, we can see that the flower essence selection is a process that involves both analytic and intuitive approaches, using both receptive listening and analytic discernment in arriving at the appropriate choice. Each practitioner creates a proper blending of the analytic and intuitive modes according to his or her temperament and that of the clients.

Bach and FES Essences

All of the practitioners interviewed began their flower essence work with the Bach Flower Remedies (the 38 essences developed in England in the 1930's) and then later added the new FES essences to their repertories. Each of the practitioners used essences from both sets, yet differed considerably about whether the Bach and FES essences should be used together. Dr. Jerome generally prefers the clarity of administering a single essence, so the issue of combining only occasionally comes up. In cases where she does combine several essences, she does not mix the Bach and FES essences in deference to the request of John Ramsell, curator of the Bach Centre in England, that they be kept separate. Dr. Smudde also reports that he uses two sets of essences in separate bottles, following his own guidance. However, the other four practitioners reported that they often combined essences from each set as determined by individual need. Dr. Andrews particularly emphasized that he perceived the essences to be "very compatible." He comments that, "there is too much separation in this world. Flowers seem compatible in Nature, they seem to get along with each other. I have seen no reason whatsever not to mix them."

Many of the practitioners volunteered comparisons of the Bach and FES essences based on their experiences. Dr. Smudde interpreted the Bach essences to be working primarily on the mental-emotional level, with the FES essences being used for higher spiritual levels, although this was not an exclusive category. Dr. Jerome characterized the differences she observed by reporting that "the Bach essences seem to fill deficiencies in people . . . whereas the FES expand or build on the character." She uses the Bach essences more for people who are ill or out of balance, while the FES essences are used for those who are fairly well but would like to achieve further evolution of their character.

Dr. Andrews, working in Monterey, California, finds that the use of the local essences enhances the experiences of his patients. For instance he relates, ". . . I might mention Sticky Monkeyflower and someone will relate a childhood story, or some experience that she or he already had with the flower, without actually knowing it could be used as a remedy. So, when I investigate further, I find that people have certain affinities with flowers anyway . . . Patients sometimes bring wildflowers like Scotch Broom or California Poppy . . . Then we start talking about the properties or effects of different remedies, and it starts to bring things up . . ."

Yet we have also found that practitioners outside of California are making extensive use of the FES essences. Rebecca Spatola now teaches classes in Europe about the essences. Suleman Aberman, as director of the

Polarity Center in Boston, reports that of the flower essences he now administers, approximately 95% are FES essences, including a number of special research essences with which he works. He notes a "slower," more basic vibration in the Bach essences which corresponds to "an earlier stage in societal process." He feels that the kind of clientel with which he works in the Boston area need the "greater differentiation between subtle vibrations" which the FES essences provide. By contrast, he also travels frequently to Montreal, Canada, and he finds that a significantly higher number of his clients there are often in need of the Bach essences.

Dr. Cindrich, working in New York City, comments that the "planetary vibration has changed since Dr. Bach did his work." Yet he finds that the differences between the two groups of essences seem less distinct when he applies the FES affirmations and the transformational work taught by Suzanne Garden (director of the Flower Essence Training Institute). So, while it appears that the new FES essences have qualities which are directly related to contemporary issues, the Bach essences still speak in a fundamental and powerful way, especially as we expand our understanding of their applications.

Counseling and Essences

Most practitioners administer flower essences in a context of counseling, although there are instances wherein the essences are given without any explanation. Suleman Aberman discusses the essences with his clients, and keeps in close communication with them after the session, inviting them to make contact if any questions or problems come up. Dr. Jerome makes a point of explaining the essences to her patients ("even with my dog"), and has them work with the affirmations from the FES journal *(issue #2, pages 12-15)*. She often uses a creative process of expanding or adapting the affirmations to meet the specific needs of a situation. For example, she added an affirmation to the Morning Glory essences that, "I greet each day with eagerness to live God's will."

". . . work with the client's awareness in a gentle way . . . It's a T'ai Chi game . . ."

Dr. Cindrich also gives each client an affirmation, but reports that the amount of counseling he does varies extensively from one individual to another. He gets considerable feedback from some clients and with others there is very little discussion, at least in the initial stages. Dr. Smudde stresses the importance of the verbal consultation in "moving things from unconsciousness to consciousness." His insight is that quite often when a practitioner avoids discussing an issue, "it is the practitioner's fear rather than the patient's fear to deal with it," especially with regard to such issues as sexuality. However, he points out that it is essential "to work with the client's awareness in a gentle way . . . It's a T'ai Chi game. You have to dance with them where they are until they are ready to get off their stuff and move on."

Dr. Andrews takes a different approach, believing that explanations can often create expectations that distort the effects of the essences, or cause an individual to dwell on the descriptions of the essences, particularly the negative aspects. Thus, he discusses the subject of flower essences in general, but does not tell his clients which essences they are taking, unless they request an explanation. In this way, he is better able to determine that the essences themselves are having an effect, rather than the person's belief or expectation about them. (This method, in effect, creates a single-blind study.)

Rebecca Spatola, on the other hand, sees the naming of the essences as a healing process in itself. Both Aberman and she have experimented with simply using the *thought* of an essence or its name as a way to evoke its energy pattern. (Of course, this method involves an initial attunement on the part of the practitioner with the specific essence.) In addition to explaining which essences are given and why, Rebecca Spatola has her clients and students meditate with photographs of flowers, and place essences on various parts of the body or in an energy field around the body, often forming particular patterns such as a triangle, a cross or a Seal of Solomon.

YARROW

Penelope Holbin

The "Healing Crisis"

Just as the practitioners differed in their blending of verbal and non-verbal approaches to flower essences, so they also had varying attitudes about the phenomena of the "healing crisis," or "awareness crisis." In describing this experience, Spatola comments that it often seems as if the client's "problem is enlarged, although in reality it has simply become closer to conscious knowledge in the process of healing itself . . . anyone who has done extensive growth work is well aware of the process of meeting and passing through the shadow of sickness in order to regain health and strength." On the other hand, Dr. Andrews feels that the term "healing crisis" should be avoided, as this may produce unnecessary anxiety in itself. His approach is ". . . to move through these things as subtly and gently as possible, without causing any further undue stress or strain." He reports that he has "never had any negative experiences with any Bach or California remedy," and that he administers an average of 15 essences a day in addition to refills.

". . . the intention of the practitioner and the expectations created . . . are extremely important influences . . ."

From these reports and from other feedback we have received from practitioners, it appears that the intention of the practitioner, and the expectation created in his or her communication with the client, are extremely important influences in how the client will experience the essences which are given. Skillfully handled, the intensification of awareness, or the "healing crisis," can be a pathway to much transformation and growth. Yet, practitioners should take care not to encourage undue expectations of cathartic upheaval, and realize that the essences have their unique, subtle way of assisting growth and release of negativity.

Experiences with Essences

When we asked these practitioners which essences seemed most prominent in their practices, we again saw the individuality of approaches. Dr. Andrews noted that Sticky Monkeyflower was used quite extensively in his practice, with uniformly excellent results. He commented that not all clients had explicitly sexual problems, but that this essence dealt with the integration of energy involved in this "basic drive." Other essences used frequently in his practice included Borage, Madia and Chamomile, the latter found to be especially helpful for children. For people more sensitive on intuitive levels, he

observed the California Poppy and Shasta Daisy to be especially helpful. Rebecca Spatola reported making frequent use of the Pink Yarrow, Blackberry and Goldenrod Bud at the time of the interview. Dr. Michael Cindrich commented that he used Red Clover extensively; he interpreted the essence as helping people recognize their own "personal doomsday fears" as well as more global anxieties. Dr. Jerome shared some of her personal favorites, including Iris for overcoming feelings of limitation about fasting, Star Tulip to assist her listening ability with music, Morning Glory for positive thought upon arising and Yarrow as a general protection while traveling.

". . . definite cycles in the use of flower essences . . ."

One of the most intriguing reports we received was from Suleman Aberman, who has discovered that there are definite cycles in the use of flower essences among his clientel. For example, during times of great social and political upheaval, he has noticed that many clients need Red Clover, Yarrow or Pink Yarrow. There were also correlations with the seasons. In spring, as there is a release of the "buried" energies of winter, he uses essences such as Sticky Monkeyflower, Scarlet Monkeyflower and Fuschsia. In the more expansive time of summer, he finds that people ". . . need help assimilating, or sorting out, balancing and staying grounded." Essences such as Dill, Manzanita, and Madia are useful as well as more purifying essences such as Sagebrush. Aberman describes autumn as a time of ". . . contracting, growing old . . . coming to terms with death." He has found that essences such as Iris and Borage are called for more often at these times. In the winter, essences which provide catalytic and fiery energy such as Cayenne and Garlic seem more often indicated. For long-range and deep spiritual work, Aberman finds the Bleeding Heart essence important for "forgiving and cleansing" as well as the Lotus essence for spiritual opening and integration. *(Cayenne, Garlic, Bleeding Heart and Lotus essences are part of the FES Research Kit.)*

Combinations

Essences can also be used in particular combinations for specific purposes. Dr. Jerome describes three personal combinations she uses for specialized activities in her life. For massage, she uses a combination of Madia, Star Tulip, Manzanita and Self-Heal. She, as well as her clients, take this combination internally at the time of bodywork, and she also applies the essences to her hands and to the skin of her clients. Dr. Jerome explains that, "Madia is for concentration . . . to bring the person's consciousness right to the part of the body being treated. Manzanita is for being in the body and not drifting . . . Self-Heal is for stimulating the body's own power to heal itself, and Star Tulip is for general receptivity and sensitivity."

As a professional cellist, Dr. Jerome takes a mixture of Borage for courage, Iris for overcoming feelings of limitation, Star Tulip for sensitivity and intonation, and Madia for concentration and memory. She also has a "meditation mixture" which she takes each morning, consisting of Shasta Daisy, Sunflower and Madia.

Dr. Smudde reports that his clinic in Los Angeles makes very extensive use of a combination of essences which they have labeled, "The Big Three," Scarlet Monkeyflower, Sticky Monkeyflower and Yarrow. "I want a person to start getting in touch with their feelings about sexuality, love and fear . . . I am trying to get them to see that as they create their universe, they create their relationships," comments Dr. Smudde. The clinic starts nearly all patients on this formula, getting them in touch with nearly-universal fears about sexuality and love. The action of the essences is assisted by counseling and then other essences are selected as specific issues surface.

Another combination used by Dr. Smudde is Yarrow and Shasta Daisy with the occasional addition of Red Clover. Dr. Smudde finds this formula useful for "psychic protection" and for those who have been manipulated or controlled by other. Dr. Smudde considers this to be a major issue as individuals evolve spiritually and open up to issues of free will and freedom of choice.

We are also continuing to receive very positive reports regarding Suzanne Garden's "manifestation formula" of Blackberry, Madia and Shasta Daisy *(described in issue #3, page 15)* as an effective tool for focusing the will and realizing goals.

Many more combinations are possible, and the preceding ones are only suggestions which can serve as examples to other practitioners to be creative in the use of essences. We do advise limiting the number of essences in a combination to no more than three or four, except in rare circumstances.

Penelope Holbin

Other Uses of Essences

Another innovative way in which essences are being used is with groups. Suleman Aberman selects essences for an entire group to take when he offers health practitioner training programs. The essences are based on the needs of that particular group and the intention of the seminar. For longer programs, he starts the whole group with common essences and, as the program continues, individuals begin getting their own essences as the specific issues of their unique individual growth process become more clear. A small group within the training program is specifically responsible for monitoring the use of essences by others and in assessing when an individual is ready for a new essence combination.

Rebecca Spatola reports that she "clears the group aura" by choosing certain essences at the beginning of a class. She reports placing flower essences in certain areas of a room to clear "psychic dust." She also describes working with essences based on "energy contained in pictures, photographs, and such written materials as letters and books," in order to get more information in the diagnosis of a particular client.

". . . as we work with flower essences our sensitivity to the subtle world increases . . ."

From these examples it becomes evident that as we work with flower essences, our sensitivity to the subtle world increases, and we can transcend conventional definitions of time and space. In this manner flower essences become a doorway into a more universal dimension. Suleman Aberman aptly describes essences as "vibrational interlocks, fields within which a practitioner and client interact . . ." He goes on to summarize that, ". . . essences are very important in sensitizing me and the people I work with to that vibrational world, and the world behind the vibrational world."

Spirit and Earth

Dr. Smudde points to the spiritual dimension in health as the area in which flower essences are particularly significant. Spiritual health, he explains, "is the responsibility of the patient while in physical form. We incarnate in physical form to serve a purpose . . . The first priority we have is raising or elevating our body, mind and spirit to our Maker. To do that, we have to make ourselves compatible to the universe we create." Dr. Smudde observes that this world includes relationships, work and the total life circumstances which we have manifested

and which evolve as our energy is elevated. So, Dr. Smudde explains that, ". . . the flower essences, as I see them, help that evolutionary path, help us move closer to creating the universe that we need to get ourselves closer to that Almighty Spirit."

". . . I don't find too many people getting well who have not forgiven those who have offended them."

In describing this evolutionary path, Dr. Smudde refers to a "Love Scale," moving from selfishness to selflessness. Few of us would be completely in the "selfless" category, but it is our goal along the spiritual path to move in that direction, and the essences are an aid to that movement. A key element, Dr. Smudde finds, is conscious recognition of one's behaviour and the ability to forgive. He comments that, "I don't find too many people getting well who have not forgiven those who have offended them."

Although Dr. Smudde developed these insights from his own experiences with the essences, readers of Dr. Bach's *Heal Thyself* (which Dr. Smudde had not read at the time of the interview), will recognize a commonality with Dr. Bach's philosophy. In this pioneering treatise on the spiritual dimensions of health, the originator of the Bach Flower Remedies spoke of the essential harmony between the personality and the soul, and the need to harmonize with the principle of Universal Love, or Unity. As in 1931 when Bach wrote *Heal Thyself,* these principles remain the foundation of our work with flower essences, and indeed of all who seek wholeness of body, mind and spirit.

". . . the essences inspire an awareness of our relationship with the living matter of Earth."

As Dr. Smudde describes the relationship of flower essences and Spirit, Dr. Andrews reminds us of how the essences inspire an awareness of our relationship with the living matter of Earth. "When people are taking essences," he comments, "they become more aware and sensitive to the earth. When people take essences, they have a more subtle appreciation of nature. I try to tell them that the next time they walk through the wilderness somewhere, to tread a bit more lightly on the earth. Taking essences and herbs helps put energy back into the earth."

"I wish you great progress in all your work, which I consider of great importance at this time, when the world as a whole is entering on a very dire time of trial, which will test all the forces of good to the uttermost; these divinely given flower essences may well be vital to our very survival, as we shall undoubtedly be up against and assailed not only by physical forces but, more importantly, by adverse forces on psychic and spiritual planes."

Dr. Aubrey T. Westlake
author and researcher in vibrational medicine

FLOWER ESSENCES AND ANIMALS:
An Interview With Richard Pitcairn, D.V.M., Ph.D.

by Patricia Kaminski

Richard Pitcairn

Several months ago, FES Co-Director, Patricia Kaminski, interviewed Dr. Richard Pitcairn, a wholistic veterinarian practicing in the Santa Cruz area and a member of the Flower Essence Society. Dr. Pitcairn is also a widely known and respected columnist for Prevention *magazine, writing a column entitled, "Your Healthy Pet." A book written by Dr. Pitcairn and Susan Hubble Pitcairn will soon be released by Rodale Press entitled,* The Complete Book of Natural Pet Care: Dogs and Cats. *The book is a comprehensive coverage of wholistic therapies for animals, and includes a section on homeopathic preparations and flower essences.*

In the following interview with Dr. Pitcairn, the underlying cultural framework which surrounds our attitudes and beliefs about animals is explored. What emerges is a deepened understanding and respect for the emotional world of animals and perhaps more importantly, a clearer view of our own human perceptions and relationships with animals. It becomes clear that flower essences can be used not only to help animals with their emotional world, but also to give deeper insight into our relationships with animals and what this reveals about our own inner life. Moreover, such wholistic approaches as flower essences actually provide a new and compelling moral alternative to the animal mode of research, which continues to introduce and extend suffering to animals as a way of researching human disease.

—Ed.

KAMINSKI: To begin with, can you provide some information on your background and how you became involved in veterinary practice?

PITCAIRN: I grew up in Los Angeles and I always liked having many animals around—I had many pets. I liked the vitality, the inherent beauty of all animals. From early on I had an idealistic vision of working with animals in some way. I graduated from veterinary school at the University of California at Davis in 1965. From there I went to a mixed practice (treating large and small animals) in southern California. I was not satisfied and did not feel I was getting many favorable results so I decided to return to school. I eventually took a job as an instructor in large animal medicine at Washington State University. While there I was offered a National Institute of Health Fellowship, so I began my Ph.D. program. By 1972 I had completed my Ph.D. in immunology and virology with a minor in biochemistry. I was doing some teaching and research with a focus on viruses and tissue cultures. For all of the investigation I had done, I was still unable to feel satisfied with the conceptual framework of the profession. What I was really interested in was what regulated an individual's ability to withstand disease and respond to it. I began to investigate the field of nutrition on my own. The changes began first within myself—I became a vegetarian and I became much more aware of natural foods and supplements.

K.: Before you applied this to animal care?

P.: Yes. All of the adaptations and insights I have made throughout my practice as a veterinarian have always started with me. The more I have known myself and my own needs as an individual, the more I have been able to understand and apply these concepts of healing to the animals I have treated.

K.: So what happened as you began to change?

P.: I stayed as a member of the faculty and taught in the university, but after a couple of years I moved. I went to

> "To use flower essences requires sensitivity, receptivity and a careful observation of the true conditions that exist. In other words, the consciousness of the user is constantly expanded and deepened through these approaches. That which is used for healing is something which itself comes from Creation. As human beings we find it and test it on ourselves, and then share the knowledge with other creatures. Such forms of medicine work in the deepest way to counteract suffering and the negativity which exists not only in our realm, but in the animal world as well. The flower essences become a way of uniting ourselves with all life on the planet and sharing that life with other living beings."

Oregon and got a job working in a small animal practice with a group of veterinarians. I began using some new applications of nutrition along with orthodox methods but I did not have a favorable situation for my work. I tended to be given cases that were already hopeless or chronic. Eventually I left that position and engaged in a variety of practices on the West Coast. I began to feel rather cynical and discouraged because I felt there wasn't an opportunity for me to express my own approach. I left the profession for a year and took a job teaching at a Quaker high school. It was revealing for me to see that I encountered the same sense of frustration and limitation in my teaching position. I began to realize that I could not leave my problems behind me. I relocated in Santa Cruz and began working on a limited basis at the SPCA clinic outside Monterey. In my spare time I began to evolve my own practice, using natural modalities of healing, and this continues to grow up to the present day. I also began writing a column for *Prevention* magazine and have come into contact with many persons throughout the country who are seeking natural and healthful solutions in pet care.

K.: Looking back on your training as a veterinarian, do you have any insights regarding the underlying cultural values and philosophical orientation of this profession?

P.: In preface I should say that veterinarians model themselves after the human medical profession. There is the prestige of being a doctor and being esteemed in the community. The kind of work is very much the same as far as training, surgery and knowledge of drugs. As a group, the veterinary profession bases its philosophy on the idea that disease is the result of some sort of disturbance from *without* the individual—the allopathic model. Disease is something that happens because something gets *into* the body—a germ, microbe, virus, etc. It almost entirely focuses on external or exterior events. What the individual is experiencing from *within* in terms of susceptibility and resistance and in emotional and mental states tends to be regarded as insignificant.

K.: Is there any move at this time in the profession toward alternative points of view?

P.: Not as a group, but there are positive trends. Most significantly there appears to be an increased recognition of nutrition. Nutritional awareness seems to be a primary point of re-orientation and re-evaluation in arriving at new concepts in health. There develops an awareness that something as common and basic as food can have a significant impact on health. This is very different from the emphasis in veterinary school which is concerned with pathology—microbes and germs and viruses and treating them with drugs.

K.: Do you see an alternative—a "wholistic" veterinary school?

P.: Practically speaking, some new ideas may gradually be adopted in the profession, and the curriculum in the schools may be modified somewhat. But I don't think things would change in a *fundamental* sense unless we have an entirely different approach and a much broader philosophical basis, one that would be based on different ethics and a very different cultural basis.

K.: Let's explore some of these values. In your articles you have written that animals have very real emotional and intellectual faculties. Yet many people respond to animals as though they could not think or feel, or if so only on a very limited basis.

P.: It is overwhelmingly true that animals have emotional states and feelings. If one is close to animals it can be seen clearly, yet it is not something that people ought to be convinced of intellectually; they must see for themselves. There is no question in my mind that animals experience the same range of emotions as people: love, fear, anger, sadness, grief, joy and so forth.

K.: Is there a difference between animals and people?

P.: Certainly there is a difference, but it is a difference in function, not necessarily one in value. As humans we tend to exaggerate emotion with our thinking process. Often when there is an emotional flare-up in a human, it is the beginning of a process which extends to all of the past hurts experienced. An animal may show anger but it is over in a few minutes and it passes.

"It is overwhelmingly true that animals have emotional states and feelings."

K.: Why do we hold emotion longer?

P.: We hold it because we do something with it and animals don't. In other words we have the capacity for symbolic thinking and logic and animals do not. We are able to perform many abstract functions which involve a tremendously active memory. Of course this ability to reason and think abstractly can have a very positive value in the whole of things. But there are some dangers, too. We tend to put things into abstract terms. We symbolize experience and in doing so we often move away from the experience itself. Let's consider the emotional state of reverence; a sense of grandeur or belonging to the whole of life. An animal would experience such a state directly through the movement of life, by being immediately in it. A typical human response toward this same emotional state might be to take a picture of it or to in some way capture or abstract it.

K.: Should we regard the human condition as inferior?

P.: There is no need to make a comparison. We have a different function within the planet and the real challenge of the human being is to be able to live with that ability without subverting it—without getting caught up in our abstractions and memories and losing the moment-to-moment direct experience of life. And this does not mean either that we must enter the animal world. What it *does* mean is that we should cultivate a respect for their unique way of consciousness. We can strive to learn from the animal world, and in deepening our understanding we also strengthen and balance our way as humans.

K.: In the current state of affairs on the planet, we have established ourselves as having power *over* animals. Our ability to function abstractly has allowed us to build a technology that gives brutal power over animals.

P.: It is not only towards animals, but is part of a larger imbalance. We treat animals as we do each other. We have hierarchies in our society, whether it be the husband dominating a wife, a parent dominating a child or a country dominating the world. For many, animals are at the bottom of the list. They cannot speak and we assume they do not have feelings. We think it doesn't matter what their sensibilities are because *we* have decided that their value is low in comparison to ours, so much so that we have decided how they shall live, what areas they shall live in, how many or few there shall be and so forth. We have decided all of these things for them.

K.: Yet we have taken certain animals such as dogs and cats and glorified them. Social critics point out that we spend more money on pet food in America than many people spend for food in other parts of the globe.

"We can strive to learn from the animal world . . . and balance our way as humans."

P.: Yet this also is part of the imbalance. While we have alienated ourselves from the world of animals, we also attempt to connect with the vital energy that animals represent. We reach out to our pets for emotional gratification in an attempt to fill that which is found absent in our culture.

K.: Can you elaborate on this emotional need?

P.: I don't know if that's the best word—many persons perceive it as a need. In other words they are lonely and they are not being satisfied in other areas. I have often noted that where there is a distortion in the relationship between a pet and its owner, there is also an imbalance in other primary relationships with that human being and other human beings. As human beings, we are meant to relate to each other and yet for many in our society it is not that way at all. Many people are afraid to find the kind of relationship that they really need with other human beings and so they turn to pets.

K.: There is security in such a relationship?

P.: There is often security because the animal is not in a position to decide whether it is to be owned or controlled. With an animal one can have a great extent of control. Most animals are taken as pets when they are quite young so that they will imprint on people at a very young age. In other words the animal lives in isolation from its own kind and identifies with people instead. If you have studied wolf packs or coyotes you know that they are social animals.

They have a communication and a sharing of experiences; mating, hunting and so forth. For this whole, rich life we substitute that of spending time with a human being.

K.: Are there any positive aspects to such a relationship that you have seen? Are there any ethical codes that you can offer?

P.: To begin with, we must understand that we need to take responsibility for the animals we have already domesticated. Most dogs and cats would no longer be able to live in the wild and certainly the alternative is not to allow packs of homeless animals to roam through the streets. The situation has changed from what it was for them in the wild state. They are living for all practical purposes in isolation from their own kind and imprinting very strongly on people. They do not perform many of their own natural instincts. They are not hunting, they are not socially interacting with their own habitat. In many instances they are not mating because they have been neutered as a necessity. Much has been taken out of their lives that has been there before and we must ask ourselves, "What is it that they have in exchange?" Let us consider the very common situation of someone who gets a large watchdog because they are afraid of burglars. So the dog lives on a chain in the back yard eating Purina Chow. Can this be compared to the rich life its ancestors lived?

"... the animal is an individual that has the potential for much growth ..."

K.: Some would say that the animal does not know any better—that it was born and raised that way.

P.: But the *potential* is there for a different life than that. We must consider that the animal is an individual that has the potential for much growth in *every* way.

K.: So our moral basis for acting is from that same foundation of love that we would extend to any being?

P.: Yes. An animal is an individual that has feelings. From the very beginning the premises can be different. There is a beautiful book entitled *Kinship With All Life* by J. Allen Boone which describes the unique experience that this man achieved as he learned to regard his dog as a teacher and equal. The author talks of the deep spiritual experiences that he and his dog achieved as they broke down the barriers between them. They were actually able to meditate together. We must ask ourselves, "What can I do to further this being's evolution as well as my own?" In other words, the question is not how that being can serve me by

keeping intruders out, satisfying my emotional needs with attention and obedience, and so forth. Rather, what does this particular individual require for its well-being and how am I responsible?

"... the way we relate to animals tells us something of the way we relate to others."

K.: That is beautifully stated. So as we get in touch with an animal's inner life and perceptions, we are also getting in touch with ourselves and our ability to love another being freely and openly?

P.: Exactly so. As I said earlier, the way we relate to animals tells us something about the way we relate to others. Can we have a relationship with an animal without false expectations? Not that the pet can do anything it wants or is left to roam aimlessly on the streets. Rather an attitude that does not dominate. This means a relationship in the sense of no exploitation and this is the same thing we strive for in our relationships with other humans, be they our children, a spouse or a friend.

K.: It's clear from what you describe that flower essences can play a significant role in the expansion of such consciousness. Have you ever administered essences to the human as well as the animal in cases you have treated?

P.: That would be an ideal circumstance but there is not the receptivity for it. It is true that the pet often mirrors the mental and emotional state of its owner or that there is a symbiotic relationship. I have had a chance to do verbal counseling with some of my clients. I will often tell people that I believe their mental state is affecting the animal, I will talk to them in terms of their own fear. We also have to realize that as I spoke earlier, the potential in many animals is not realized and so they are very attached and dependent on people. Let's say a woman gets a dog or cat because she is living alone or that she gets a pet rather than having a child in a marriage relationship. As you can imagine that animal is the recipient of a tremendous amount of emotional input. There is the focus of attention, not only physically but emotionally. Many things happen on a telepathic level. The animal picks up all sorts of things from the person and reflects what is happening.

K.: Can you give an example of this?

P.: For instance, there may be a couple living together and they have a cat. All of the sudden there is a lot of

emotional conflict and they break up and the cat goes with one of them. It's not unusual for a cat to get sick in such a situation—I have seen it happen many times. There is a great deal of tension plus the added stress of a move. All of the sudden the cat is sick and the veterinarian diagnoses him as "leukemia positive," or some other "disease entity."

"...the pet often mirrors the mental and emotional state of its owner..."

K.: Let's focus then on your actual treatment of animals and how you use the flower essences. I also know you use other wholistic methods of healing. Could you give us an overview of your approach?

P.: There are many modalities that are possible and I have focused on a few of them that work well for me. I almost always have nutritional advice to give because I feel strongly that animals fed commercial food are very under-nourished. I usually take them off commercial food and put them on a diet of cooked grains, some vegetables, fresh meat, dairy products and supplements such as yeast, cod liver oil, bone meal and vegetable oil. Many animals also need a cleansing diet and need to avoid toxic foods—including organ meats which can be highly toxic if fed in excess. In addition to this basic approach I usually include one of three methods: homeopathic medications, tissue (cell) salts or the flower essences. Sometimes I do use herbs, but if I do I tend to use them in homeopathic preparation because they are so much more potent in this form.

K.: By what methods do you make your selection?

P.: I use whatever will give me real information. When I see the animal I am interested in how it moves around, what behavioral patterns are evident and how the animal appears. I might look at the skin and give a quick physical exam but I am not as interested in doing lab tests and that sort of thing as the usual veterinarian does. If they need that I recommend they go somewhere else. I also devote a lot of attention to the history and symptoms of the animal as described by the person. Additionally, I ask for a history from the human(s) involved, what's been happening in his/her life. All of this takes an hour and a half or longer on the first visit. That is not regarded as lucrative from a professional standpoint but I feel it's extremely necessary in order to get the information I need. By the time I have gathered this information, I usually have a pretty good idea both intuitively and intellectually about what to do.

K.: When are the flower essences most often indicated?

P.: A general guideline I use is that it seems flower essences work well when there is a very clear mental or emotional component. Let's say a couple breaks up and the cat goes with one of them. In that case, if the animal has gotten ill, regardless of the kind of physical illness it has, there is almost always an element of shock involved. In such cases I will use Star of Bethlehem either alone or in formula. Perhaps a baby has been born into a family where the pet previously had all of the attention—Chicory is often indicated in such situations. I find that Chicory is generally useful for many dogs. In their relationships there is often an element of wanting to possess a person and of getting attention — a feeling of self-pity, if I can put it in human terms. Or let's say an animal is very aggressive or vicious, I might use Holly or Beech.

"I find that Chicory is generally useful for many dogs..."

K.: Are there any specific guidelines for using flower essences beyond this general one?

P.: Yes. I often use flower essences for animals that are very old or very weak and have severe diseases and are perhaps close to death. I also use them in very young animals—little puppies, kittens and birds. Finally, I use the essences very often on animals that have had a lot of drug treatment. I find the flower essences extremely useful where the vitality has been severely weakened, although I am not sure why. I also find the essences sometimes work in cases where the animal has been drugged (with cortisone for instance), whereas homeopathic medications are often inactivated by other drugs.

K.: Do you use the flower essences for animals that are generally in good health?

P.: As I indicated, if there is a clear cut emotional or mental state I sometimes do. Most often though, I use the homeopathic medications. For instance, I have found that skin problems are very chronic and are often associated with many internal physical imbalances. I have found that I get more definite results for these kinds of symptoms using homeopathic preparations. Perhaps this is because the problem has such a physical focus. I can get much better and faster results at this point than I can with something like Crab Apple for general cleansing.

K.: What procedures do you recommend for administering the flower essences to animals?

P.: I have put them in the mouth of the animal just as one would for a person, four times a day. Sometimes I recommend fewer drops if the animal is quite small. One can also put the essences in the animal's drinking water—this works well if the animal is being treated and the person must be gone for the day. However, this method is not the most reliable since one is not sure whether or how often the water has been drunk. If the condition is very serious I will have the essences administered every one or two hours.

> "... flower essences work well when there is a very clear mental or emotional component."

K.: Can you share a case study which has involved the use of flower essences?

P.: As an example, I treated a cat with a rather serious disorder called Feline Infectious Peritonitis. I did not really know, at first, what approach to take with this case. As a temporary measure, I used a flower essence formula to strengthen the animal even though I did not anticipate that a cure would result. After a few days, there was some improvement and as the energy level went up, the symptoms became more prominent and I was able to recognize the appropriate homeopathic remedy required. All other treatment was then stopped and the homeopathic treatment administered. One dose was sufficient to bring about recovery in a few weeks. We have administered two more treatments of one dose each over the last year as the symptoms have returned. The improvement in the animal is startling! Behavior has changed, general health has improved, and several pounds of weight gained. In this case, I feel that the initial treatment with the flower essence was helpful in setting the stage for the response seen. I would also like to add that Rescue Remedy is used as a standard treatment for animals that have been injured, or have received surgery or are in shock in some way (though I more often use Arnica). We literally have brought some animals back from death with Rescue Remedy. It does not work indefinitely, however. Rescue Remedy gets the animal over the initial shock and then after a few hours something else is needed to finish the case.

K.: Do you have any other comments you wish to make about flower essences as a healing modality?

P.: To me one of the most exciting things about flower essences and homeopathy is that whether people currently understand it or not, they are superior forms of medicine in every respect. Perhaps there is still a place for more orthodox methods like surgery, particularly when we are talking about injuries or accidents. But when compared with drugs and other allopathic approaches, the flower essences and homeopathy are highly efficacious. The more I learn about these alternative approaches, the more outstanding results I am able to get (and there is much I am still learning). Secondly, in an ethical or moral sense there is much to be said for this form of healing. In our current culture, we have a model which asserts that disease is something which afflicts us from without and hasn't much to do with our inner state. Then we feel that we can solve the problem of these diseases by deliberately introducing them into animals where we can study them in isolation from ourselves. We are going to observe this disease in the animal and then to cut the animal open and take tissue cultures and so forth. In other words, one of the most terrible and often over-looked aspects of this kind of medicine is that it creates what is called an "animal model" in research. There is a tremendous amount of money and work going into that. So if we have heart disease in people we will create heart disease in pigs so that we can have a model to observe. Then we are going to get down to more and more detail until we have finally found what we assume to be causing it—a microbe, a virus, or some sort of piece of RNA or DNA. Then we develop a drug to counteract this and once again we return to the animals to experiment with the drug. We introduce the drug into so many thousands of diseased animals until we find a drug that seems to be effective in controlling the symptoms. Then we gingerly apply the technique to more "valuable" human life.

> "... in an ethical or moral sense there is much to be said for this form of healing."

K.: So although the goal of medicine is to alleviate suffering, the animal model of research actually extends suffering into places it had not been before?

P.: Yes, we are actually introducing suffering in thousands of living beings. We are forcing organisms to encounter disease where it has never been before. We are creating genetic mutations in animal life and so forth. But the ray of hope is to consider the natural forms of medicine such as homeopathy and flower essences. To use flower essences requires sensitivity, receptivity, and a careful observation of the true conditions that exist. In other words, the consciousness of the user is constantly expanded and deepened through these approaches. That which is used for healing is something which itself comes from Creation. As human beings, we find it and we test in on *ourselves* and then we share this knowledge with other creatures. Such forms of medicine work in the deepest way to counteract the suffering and the negativity which exists, not only in our realm, but in the animal world as well. The flower essences become a way of uniting ourselves with all of life on the planet and sharing that life with other living beings.

References

Dr. Pitcairn suggests the following books as further references regarding concepts discussed in this article:

Bach, Edward. *Heal Thyself: An Explanation of the Real Cause and Cure of Disease.* London: C. W. Daniel Co., Ltd., 1931. *See especially Chapter VI in which is discussed use of animals in research.*

Boone, J. Allen. *Kinship With All Life.* New York: Harper and Row, 1954.

Boone, J. Allen. *The Language of Silence.* New York: Harper and Row, 1970.

Chancellor, Phillip. *Handbook of the Bach Flower Remedies.* London: C. W. Daniel Co., Ltd., 1971.

Hamlyn, Edward, M.D. *The Healing Art of Homeopathy.* New Haven, Connecticut: Keats Publishing Co., 1979. *This is a new interpretation of Hahnemann, the founder of homeopathy, in a style fairly easy to read.*

Singer, Peter. *Animal Liberation: A New Ethics for our Treatment of Animals.* New York: Avon Books, 1975.

Tanzer, Herbert, D.V.M. *Your Pet Isn't Sick (He Just wants You to Think So).* New York: Jove Publications, 1977.

Vithoulkas, George. *Homeopathy: Medicine of the New Man.* New York: Arco Publishing Co., 1979. *This is an excellent explanation of homeopathy.*

"On every act the balance of the whole depends. The wind and the seas, the powers of water and earth and light, all that these do, all that the beasts and green things do is well done and rightly done. All these act within the Equilibrium. From the hurricane and the great whale's sounding to the fall of a dry leaf and the gnat's flight, all they do is done within the balance of the whole. But we, in so far as we have power over the world and over one another, we must *learn* to do what the leaf and the whale and the wind do of their own nature. We must learn to keep the balance. Having intelligence, we must not act in ignorance. Having choice, we must not act without responsibility."

Ursula Le Guin
from *The Farthest Shore*

Maitreya

BOTANY OF THE BACH FLOWERS, Part IV

by Darrell Wright

The 38 Bach Flower Essences were developed by the late Dr. Edward Bach in the 1930's in England, and have been prepared there by the Bach Centre since the doctor's death in 1936. During its half-century of use, this "classical" system of essences has established a world-wide reputation for effectiveness in helping people to transform a wide range of emotional and personality patterns.

In the first three issues of this journal, Flower Essence Society botanical consultant Darrell Wright has examined the botanical characteristics of the tree and shrub species used by Dr. Bach in preparing his essences. In this concluding article in the series, he deals with the herbaceous species. —Ed.

Trees, Shrubs and Herbs

Botanists traditionally have had difficulty making a workable technical distinction between tree and shrub. The difficulty arises from the rich variability of the plants, which do not worry much about conforming to our distinctions for them. Tree species occasionally grow as shrubs, like the California Bay Tree, *Umbellulària califòrnica* Nuttall, in windswept habitats along the Pacific Coast, and shrubs like certain Manzanitas, *Arctostáphylos* species, occasionally become tree-like. The distinction between the woody plants and the herbs or herbaceous plants is an easier one. Both distinctions can be summarized with a key like the keys to plant species found in floras:

A. Woody above ground.
   B. With one large main trunk, plant usually taller than 10 feet . . . . tree
   BB. With several smaller main trunks, plant usually shorter than 10 feet . . . . shrub
AA. Not woody above ground . . . . herb
   B. With woody or fibrous roots or bulbs which persist for more than one growing season . . . . perennial herbs
   BB. With non-woody roots which die along with the rest of the plant after one growing season . . . . annual herbs

Subshrubs are woody only at the base of the stem; they have evolved nearly to the level of perennial herb. Herbs are usually, but not always, smaller than shrubs. Bach's Impatiens, an annual herb, grows to six feet, while the Common Sunflower, *Heliánthus ánnuus* Linnaeus, reaches 12 feet. We continue now with descriptions of the herbaceous species, perennial and annual, used by Dr. Bach.

The Bach Species

AGRIMONY, *Agrimònia eupatòria* Linnaeus, for those who are "restless and worried in mind or body, they hide their cares behind their humor . . ." (Bach, 1933, p. 17). Rose Family (Rosaceae). Agrimony, Common Agrimony. Instead of applying different names to this species and thereby building up a list of synonyms for it, taxonomists have applied the same name, *A. eupatoria,* to different species. Hegi (1932), for example, applies the name *A. eupatoria* to forms which both *Flora of the British Isles* (FB) and *Flora Europaea* (FE) recognize as distinct species, *A. odoràta* Miller and *A. pròcera* Wallroth. The taxonomists do the best they can, but some groups of plants cause much confusion, and it may be decades before the relationships within a group, such as the genus *Agrimonia,* are satisfactorily worked out. Weeks and Bullen (1964) give *"Agrimonia eupatoria* or *Agrimonia odorata"* at the head of the section of their book devoted to the Agrimony essence. It is not clear whether they mean that either species can be used or whether they believe the two names refer to the same species and they are in effect giving *A. odorata* as a synonym. Their illustration is labelled "A. eupatoria," and *The Twelve Healers* gives only that name in the 1977 and earlier reprintings. The scientific names have been omitted from the 1979 reprinting.

A. eupatoria is native over most of central and southern Europe where it grows on hedgebanks, roadsides at edges of fields and in waste places, behaving rather as a weed and making itself quite available. It is apparently not much cultivated here, although it should be well suited to temperate climates everywhere. (I have seen it for sale in my

AGRIMONY *Agrimonia eupatoria*

glands on the lower side of the leaflet and lacks grooves on the lower part of the fruit. Also, *A. odorata,* unlike Bach's Agrimony, is sweet smelling, probably from the glandular secretions. (*Agrimonia,* according to Lewis and Short (1879), is a misreading of *argemònia,* a possibly related herb used in early times for the treatment of *eye* disorders; *eupatoria,* because of the similarity in appearance to the sunflower genus, *Eupatòrium,* Boneset.)

CENTAURY, *Centaùrium erythraèa* Rafinesque, for those "who are over-anxious to serve others. . . . Their wish so grows upon them that they become more servants than willing helpers" (Bach, 1933, p. 17). Gentian Family (Gentianaceae). Centaury, Common Centaury. Synonyms: *C. mìnus* and *C. umbellàtum* of various authors (*C. umbellatum* is the name which appears in *The Twelve Healers*); *Erythraea centaurium* of various authors; *Gentiana centaurium* Linnaeus. *C. erythraea* is native on relatively dry sites from Sweden south and east to Southwest and Central Asia. It is present as an introduction in open fields and waste places along the immediate coast from Mendocino County, California, north to Washington, flowering June through August (Abrams, 1951; Munz, 1959; as *C. umbellatum*). Bach's Centaury is an erect annual to 20 inches in height, usually with a single stem which is branched above. Those leaves which form a rosette at the base of the stem are up to two inches long and ¾ inches wide, reverse egg-shaped or elliptic, with blunt tips and three to seven prominent nerves running the length of the leaf. The stem leaves are smaller and may have acute rather than blunt tips. The one-half inch long pink flowers are stalkless or nearly so with five one-quarter inch long pointed lobes spreading from the tubular part of the corolla at a right angle. Five stamens arise from between the lobes at the top of this tube. The anthers (pollen sacs at the top of the stamens) become spirally twisted after they split open to shed the pollen.

Bailey (1949) gives only one *Centaurium* species as cultivated in North America, a perennial quite unlike *C. erythraea.* However, the fact that Bach's species is naturalized here suggests that it would not be hard to cultivate, at least where the climate was not too hot. (*Centaurium,* the classical Latin name for this plant, whose medicinal properties are said to have been discovered by Chiron, "wisest and justest of all the Centaurs . . . renowned for his skill in hunting [and] medicine;" *erythraea,* reddish, cf. Greek *eruthròs,* red. The ending is feminine rather than neuter in agreement with *Centaurium,* because the word is a noun, in this instance the name of a genus into which the species was formerly placed. A few years ago the species name would have been capitalized to indicate that it was a noun, *C. Erythraea.*)

area among a collection of kitchen herbs.) *A. eupatoria* is a perennial herb to two feet in height, densely leafy above, sparsely so below. The lower leaves are compound with three to six pairs of large leaflets alternating with pairs of smaller leaflets. The largest leaflets are two and one-half inches long, elliptic in outline and with conspicuous marginal serration. The leaflets are hairy above and below but lack the glands which characterize the leaves of other *Agrimonia* species. The numerous yellow flowers are only one-fourth inch in diameter and are borne in an elongate cluster at the top of the stem. They have five separate petals and a variable number of stamens. The small fruits are grooved nearly from top to bottom and have hooked spines on the upper half.

A. odorata, the other species mentioned by Weeks and Bullen, resembles *A. eupatoria* but has abundant stalkless

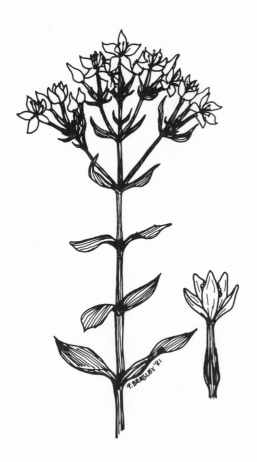

CENTAURY *Centaurium erythraea*

ing from a common receptacle which is surrounded at its base by leaflike bracts which collectively form the involucre. This arrangement (head) of flowers appears superficially as one flower, and there can be some excitement in discovering that what was taken for a single flower is actually made up of many tiny flowers called florets. In the case of Chicory, the corollas of these florets are a striking bright blue. The color is almost enough to identify the plant, if it can be recognized as a member of the Sunflower Family, as there are so few blue sunflowers. Each floret produces a single 2–3 mm. long irregularly angled seed which is pale brown, often with darker mottling.

Weeks and Bullen (1964) warn that the flowers are sensitive to the heat of the hand and fade quickly when picked. They advise accumulating no more than two or three before floating them in the bowl of water. There is also a time constraint on making the essence: the flower heads close at about midday. (*Cichorium*, classical Latin name for this plant. One source claims the word is of Arabic origin; *intybus*, another noun used as a species adjective. This is another classical Latin name for chicory or perhaps for the related endive, *C. endivia* Linnaeus.)

CHICORY, *Cichòrium ìntybus* Linnaeus, for those "who tend to be over-full of care for children, relatives, friends, always finding something that should be put right" (Bach, 1933, p. 22). Sunflower Family (Asteraceae). Chicory, Succory. The references give no synonym. *C. intybus* is native to Europe, Western Asia and North Africa and occurs as an introduction throughout most of the remainder of the planet, including North America. It is a perennial herb to nearly four feet in height with a long stout taproot by which it winters over from year to year while the above ground parts die back. The tough stems are erect, grooved and hairy. The spreading branches may lack hairs. The reverse lance-shaped leaves at the base of the stem form a rosette and have margins which may be cut more or less into lobes or may be merely toothed. The leaf margins bear gland-tipped hairs. The stem leaves above the base are lance-shaped and clasp the stem with their bases.

The flower heads of Chicory are terminal and solitary or may be two or three together in the angles (axils) where the upper branches join the stem. The heads are up to 1½ inches in diameter and of typical sunflower construction (see sketch) with many very small individual flowers grow-

CHICORY *Cichorium intybus*

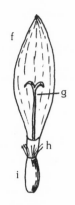

Generalized Sunflower:

a—ray floret
b—disc floret
c—disc floret bud
d—individual bracts (phyllaries)
e—receptacle
f—ray floret with single ray petal
g—style with curving stigma
h—pappus of fine bristles (a kind of calyx)
i—ovary
j—corolla of disc floret (opened to expose)
k—stamens united by their anthers
l—staminal filaments

Adapted from Munz, 1959.

GENTIAN, *Gentianélla amarélla* (Linnaeus) Börner, for "those who are easily discouraged . . . any small delay or hindrance to progress causes doubt and soon disheartens them" (Bach, 1933, p. 11). Gentian Family (Gentinaceae). Gentian, Felwort. Synonyms: *Amarella amarella* (Linnaeus) Cockerell; *A. acùta* Rydberg; *A. califôrnica, copelándii* and *lembértii* E. L. Greene; *A. plèbeja* (Chamisso) E. L. Greene; *Gentiàna acuta* Michaux; *G. amarella* Linnaeus; *G. anisosèpala* E. L. Greene; *G. axillàris* (Schmidt) Reichenbach; *G. plebeja* Chamisso ex Bunge; *G. septentrionális* (Druce) Druce; *Gentianella septentrionalis* (Druce) E. F. Warburg. All these names were almost

certainly applied with the greatest scientific precision with which these botanists were capable, yet this plant has evidently caused some confusion.

Lack of communication betweeen botanists was only part of the problem. First, there has been difficulty concerning the way in which the genus *Gentiana* should be defined. European workers feel that plants with a fringe of hairs in the corolla throat and without accessory lobes between the main corolla lobes deserve to be recognized as a genus apart from *Gentiana,* and this genus they call *Gentianella.* On the other hand, at least some American workers prefer to think of *Gentiana* as a genus containing several subgenera, one of which has two sections, Section Gentianella with the fringe of hairs and Section Gentiana without it, but they call all the species *Gentiana.* Then there is the earlier name, *Amarella,* which at some point fell by the wayside. Finally, there is the matter of so many species having been recognized. *G. amarella* is very variable, and divergent forms have tended to get named as species in their own right before more thorough study has shown that there are no consistent differences between the forms and that they are more appropriately thought of as one species. This confusing situation is illustrated by the problem of the American versus the European plants. A. H. Grisebach, a 19th century German authority on the Gentian Family, believed that North American plants called *G. amarella* were not the same species as European plants that went by that name. M. L. Fernald, distinguished taxonomist and plant geographer at Harvard University, studied the problem carefully and concluded (Fernald, 1917): "I am unable to discern any constant differences between the American and the European plant. The differences maintained by Grisebach all fail in a good series of specimens." It is now reasonably safe to say that Dr. Bach's Gentian is native both here in North America and in Europe.

G. amarella is found across Central Europe and across the northern United States and in the mountains as far south as Mexico. In California it is in the Sierra Nevada north to Siskiyou County in moist places from 4500 to 11000 feet (Munz, 1959). It is a biennial with a leafy erect stem to one or occasionally two feet in height. In the first year the plant produces a rosette of basal leaves varying from lance- to tongue-shaped. These die away in autumn, and the following summer a new rosette of basal leaves appears, reverse egg-shaped or spatulate, different from those of the first year's rosette. The stem leaves are lance-linear to egg-shaped and less than one inch long. The blue or purple flowers are about an inch long and may be on the plan of either four or five, even on the same plant, that is, there may be four or five corolla lobes and an equal number of stamens. Each corolla lobe has the characteristic fringe of hairs arising from where the lobe joins the tubular part of the corolla.

Bach's Gentian is a small, non-showy species that is evidently not much cultivated. It is not among the 24 species given by Bailey (1949) as cultivated in North America. *Sunset Western Garden Book* also does not mention *G. amarella.* It does mention that most Gentians are hard to grow, so this is probably a plant that would require special care in cultivation. (*Gentianella,* diminutive from *Gentiana,* the type genus of the Gentian Family, named for King Gentius of Illyria, who is said to have discovered Gentian's medicinal properties; *amarella,* presumably diminutive from *amárus,* bitter; the Gentians are noted for the bitter tasting substances which they contain.)

GENTIAN *Gentianella amarella*

HONEYSUCKLE, *Lonícera caprifòlium* Linnaeus, for "those who do not expect further happiness such as they have had" (Bach, 1933, p. 13). Honeysuckle Family (Caprifoliaceae). Honeysuckle. Synonyms: *L. itálica* Wood; *L. pállida* Host; *L. perfoliàta* Edwards; *L. rotundifòlia* Medicus; *L. suàvis* Salisbury. Native to Central and Southern Europe and Asia Minor and introduced in the British Isles, Bach's Honeysuckle is a woody vine like Clematis and not herbaceous. (It has to be included here instead of with the shrubs with which it belongs because of my oversight.) The stem may reach 20 feet in length. The egg-shaped or oblong leaves are up to four inches long,

dark green above and with a whitish dust or "bloom" on the lower surface. The lower leaves have stalks except for the first two or three pairs below the flower cluster, which have their bases more or less grown together so that they look like a single leaf with the stem of the plant passing through its center. The flowers are in dense terminal clusters, often with a few clusters arising from the leaf axils immediately below. The corolla is two inches long with the four upper lobes united to form an upper lip and the fifth forming a lower lip. The corolla is cream white within and purplish or yellowish outside. The fruit is an orange or red berry.

L. caprifolium is distinguished from the 26 other Honeysuckle species given by Bailey as cultivated here by having the upper leaves fused at their bases, flowers two to three or more in a cluster rather than strictly in pairs, longer than one inch, with the tubular part a little longer than the lobes.

Weeks and Bullen (1964) advise that the essence should be made by boiling entire flower clusters, including six inches of attached stem and leaves. They seem to warn against confusing Bach's Honeysuckle with Woodbine, *L. periclỳmenum* Linnaeus, which is native in the British Isles and is cultivated here. It does not have the upper leaves fused at their bases. (*Lonicera,* named for Adam Lonitzer, 1528–1586, German physician and naturalist; *caprifolium,* from *càper, capri,* goat, and *fòlium,* leaf, perhaps because this vine climbs like a goat [Bailey]).

HONEYSUCKLE *Lonicera caprifolium*

IMPATIENS *Impatiens glandulifera*

IMPATIENS, *Impàtiens glandulífera* Royle, for "those who are quick in thought and action and who wish all things to be done without delay . . . They find it very difficult to be patient with people who are slow . . ." (Bach, 1933, p. 16). Balsam Family (Balsaminaceae). Policeman's Helmet. Synonyms: *I.glandulígera* Lindley; *I. ròylei* Walpers. Bach's *Impatiens* is another species which is not native to the British Isles. It was introduced from the Himalayas and is now completely naturalized on river banks and in waste places, and, according to FB, was still increasing in 1950. Bailey (1949) gives it as naturalized in North America. This species is an erect robust annual herb which reaches six feet in height. The botanist who named it in 1839 calls it a "giant species." The stem is stout, reddish, ribbed, succulent, and almost translucent. The leaves are opposite or in whorls of three with a pair of large stalked glands at the base of the petiole (leaf stalk). They are two to six inches long, lance-shaped or elliptic with numerous marginal teeth and a red midrib. The flowers are up to 1½ inches long in clusters in the axils of the upper leaves. The lower of the three sepals is prolonged into a short hollow spur in which nectar collects. This nectar is consumed by bumble bees which pollinate the flowers in the process of getting to the spur. The four lower petals are partly united in pairs; the upper one stands free above them. Their color is purplish pink (FB) or mauve (Weeks and Bullen, 1964; pale bluish purple). The fruit is a ¾ inch long capsule which hangs down at maturity.

I. glandulifera is separated from the four other *Impatiens* species given by Bailey (1949) by having the flower clusters long-stalked with the flowers mostly towards the ends of the branches, the leaves opposite and the spur very short. (*Impatiens*, impatient, from *pàtior*, to bear, suffer, "referring to the sudden bursting of the ripe pods when touched" (Bailey); *glandulifera*, from *glándula*, kernel, gland, and *féro*, to bear, carry.)

MIMULUS, *Mímulus guttàtus* DeCandolle, for "fear of worldly things, illness, pain, accidents, poverty . . . the fears of everyday life" (Bach, 1933, p. 9). Figwort Family (Scrophulariaceae). Monkey-Flower, Speckled Monkey-Flower. Synonyms: *M. arvénsis, clementìnus, equìnus, paniculátus, petiolàris,* and *pròcerus* E. L. Greene; *M. langsdòrfii* Donn ex Greene; *M. lùteus* of English authors; *M. micránthus* Heller; *M. microphýllus* Bentham; *M. nasùtus* E. L. Greene var. *micránthus* A. Grant;

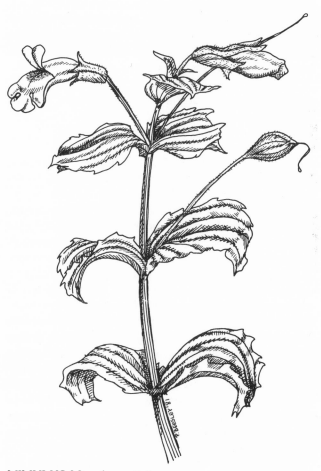

MIMULUS *Mimulus guttatus*

M. platycàlyx Pennell. Dr. Bach's Mimulus is native on the Pacific Coast of North America east to the Rocky Mountains and was introduced into Europe from here. FB says of it, "First recorded in 1830, now rather common on the banks of streams, *etc.*, through nearly the whole of the British Isles and appearing quite native." According to Hegi (v. 6:2, 1929, p. 1360), the species was spreading along water courses in continental Europe in the late twenties, and he lists new localities in which it was observed since 1918.

Mimulus is a perennial herb to three feet in height, although it does not grow this tall in the British Isles. The oval leaves have marginal teeth toward the base and are up to three inches long. The leaves on the upper stem are stalkless and more or less fused at their bases. The two-lipped yellow corolla is about 1½ inches long with the lower lip generally spotted red and the upper sometimes so. The parts of the plant associated with the flowers are usually glandular hairy. *M. guttatus,* which is naturalized also in the eastern U. S., flowers here from March through August. It is common in wet places, occurring even among the plantings around a downtown city hospital, where I saw three dozen plants come up spontaneously this year.

Bailey (1949) gives a total of 10 species in cultivation in North America among which *M. guttatus* is distinguished by being herbaceous rather than woody, by foliage that is not sticky and by yellow flowers which have the throat (entrance into the tubular lower part of the flower) closed or nearly so. (*Mimulus,* diminutive of *mìmus,* comic actor said to be because of the "grinning" corolla; *guttatus,* spotted, from *gùtta,* speck or spot.)

MUSTARD, *Sínapis arvénsis* Linnaeus, for "those who are liable to times of despair, as though a cold dark cloud overshadowed them and hid the light and joy of life" (Bach, 1933, p. 14). Mustard Family (Brassicaceae). Charlock, Wild Mustard. Synonyms: *Brássica arvensis* (Linnaeus) Rabenhorst, but not *B. arvensis* Linnaeus; *B. kàber (DeCandolle) L. C. Wheeler; B. sinapis* de Visiani; *B. sinapístrum* Boissier. (The rest of the long list of synonyms, mostly old, given by Hegi for this species will be found in his volume 4:1, p. 263, 1917.) Unlike their European colleagues, most western North American botanists have chosen not to recognize *Sinapis* as a genus distinct from *Brassica;* they treat all of these mustards as *Brassica,* whether the beak or tip of the pod is flattened and contains seeds or is conical-rounded and seedless. Thus Dr. Bach's Mustard, which is a widespread weed here, is apt to be given in western floras as *B. kaber* (DeCandolle) Wheeler. Since it is optional whether we call it *Sinapis* or *Brassica,* we stay with the name used in *The Twelve Healers.*

Sinapis arvensis is native in Europe, North Africa and Southwest Asia, and has been introduced practically

MUSTARD *Sinapis arvensis*

everywhere else. (Is the fact that this plant is so widespread related to the need for the essence of modern man, who suffers so much from depression?) It is an annual herb with an erect, usually stiffly-hairy stem to 2½ feet in height. The leaves are lyre-shaped, spreading out towards the tip with a large terminal lobe and several smaller lobes below. They may be up to eight inches long. The yellow flowers are in elongate clusters at the top of the stem. They are typical of the Mustard Family with four sepals and four equal petals suggesting a cross; the traditional name for the family, which may still be used if one wishes, is Cruciferae from *crùx, crùcis,* cross, and *féro,* to bear. The slender pointed pods which stand upright and close to the stem are also typical of the family. In the case of *S. arvensis* these are about one inch long and contain a dozen small, round, dark red-brown seeds in each of two chambers. Bailey (1949, as *B. kaber*) gives four other cultivated species in the *Sinapis* group from which Bach's species is distinguished by having the seeds small (not much more than 1 mm. in diameter), the pod at most only finely hairy, not more than 1½ inches long and pressed close to the stem at maturity. (*Sinapis,* Greek name for some Mustard Family plant; *arvensis,* of the field, *àrva.*)

ROCK ROSE, *Heliánthemum nummulàrium* (Linnaeus) Miller, for those who are "very frightened or terrified, or if the condition is serious enough to cause great fear to those around" (Bach, 1933, p. 9). Rock Rose Family (Cistaceae). Common Rock Rose, Sunrose, Hedge-Hyssop (Hegi). Synonyms: *Cístus nummularius* Linnaeus; *Helianthemum chamaecístus* Miller; *H. vulgàre* Gaertner. Rock Rose is native on limestone soil in grassy and rocky places throughout Europe and is also in Asia Minor and Iran. It is a small shrub to one foot in height with numerous branches which trail along the ground and tend to put down roots. The leaves are opposite on the stem, oblong or oval to one inch long, green above and densely white hairy below with branching hairs. The margins are smooth and the blade is supported on a short stalk (petiole). Small but plainly evident leaf-like appendages called stipules are present where the petiole joins the stem. The bright yellow flowers are in clusters at the top of the stem and are all turned to one side of the stem. The flowers are a little more than one inch in diameter with five separate sepals and petals. The three inner sepals are larger than the outer two. The ovary, which is surrounded by numerous stamens, matures into a hairy, egg-shaped capsule about one-fourth inch long.

Bach's Rock Rose is cultivated in North America, but hybrids in various colors are often sold here under the name *H. nummularium*. Weeks and Bullen (1964) write that the garden hybrids "are not used" for the essence. *H. nummularium* is separated from the five other cultivated species given by Bailey (1949) by the presence of stipules and a well developed style (slender tube atop the ovary through which pollen grows down to the ovules and fertilizes them) and unbranched hairs on the upper surfaces of the leaves. (*Helianthemum*, from Greek *hèlios*, sun, and *ánthemon*, flower; *nummularium*, pertaining to money, *nùmmus*, perhaps because of the flowers suggesting gold coins.

SCLERANTHUS *Scleranthus annuus*

SCLERANTHUS, *Scleránthus ánnuus* Linnaeus, for "those who suffer much from being unable to decide between two things, first one seeming right then the other" (Bach, 1933, p. 11). Pink Family (Caryophyllaceae). Knawel (German: *knot*; pronounced nowl). Synonyms: *S. campéstris* Schur; *S. élegans* Barth; *S. ruscinonénsis* (Gillot and Coste) P. D. Sell; *S. taùricus* Presl; *S. verticillàtus* Tausch. This diminutive annual is native to Europe, North Africa and the temperate parts of Asia. It has been introduced into North America and is sparingly naturalized in the Pacific States in places like dry fields and roadsides. The much branched stems reach 10 inches in height in Europe, while Munz (1959) gives the tallest California plants as only four inches. The leaves are narrow and pointed, one-half inch long and bear short marginal hairs. They are opposite one another on the stem and have their bases somewhat grown together. The flowers are only one-eighth to one-fourth of an inch long, solitary in the forks of the stem and in clusters in the leaf axils and at the tips of the stem. The greenish calyx tube divides into five

ROCK ROSE *Helianthemum nummularium*

pointed lobes with membranous margins which can be difficult to see. There are no petals. The ovary is surrounded by 10 or fewer stamens and is topped by two distinct styles.

The plant is not cultivated, though I am sure it could be. The seed would have to be collected from native or naturalized populations. Localities could be got from the information on herbarium sheets in college herbaria or from local floras. For example, one comes across this little note in the *Supplement* to Howell's flora of Marin County (1970): "*S. annuus* L., Knawel, a native of Europe, has been detected as an inconspicuous annual on a serpentine flat near Forest Knolls by Beecher Crampton (No. 4205)." (*Scleranthus,* from Greek *sklerós,* hard, and *ánthos,* flower, because the calyx becomes hard in fruit; *annuus,* annual, from *ánnus,* year.)

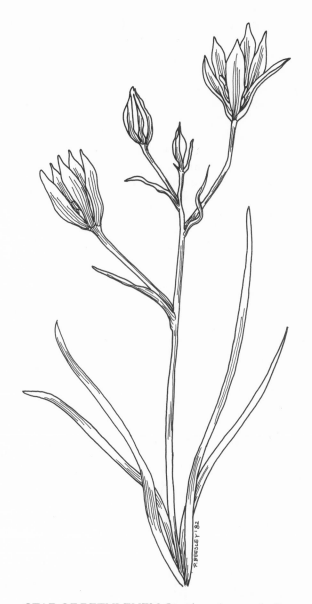

STAR OF BETHLEHEM *Ornithogalum umbellatum*

STAR OF BETHLEHEM, *Ornithogàlum umbellàtum* Linnaeus, "for those in great distress under conditions which for a time produce great unhappiness. The shock of serious news, the loss of someone dear, the fright following an accident..." (Bach, 1933, p.20). Lily Family (Liliaceae). Star of Bethlehem. Synonyms: *Scílla campéstris* Savi; *Stellàris corymbòsa* Moench.

Bach's Star of Bethlehem is typical of the monocotyledons (monocots), one of the two main groups of vascular plants (as opposed to mosses and fungi which are non-vascular, that is, without fluid bearing vessels in their tissues). The monocots are built on the plan of three, in this case six "petals" and six stamens and angles on the ovary; they put up just one initial leaf or cotyledon and have the fluid carrying vessels scattered in the tissue of the stem. The other Bach species we have examined so far, excluding the conifers, have been members of the other group, the dicotyledons (dicots), with flowers on the plan of four or five, two initial leaves and fluid carrying vessels gathered into bundles in the stem tissue. The other monocot used by Dr. Bach is the grass, *Bròmus ramòsus,* his Wild Oat.

Star of Bethlehem is native about the Mediterranean but only questionably native in the British Isles. Like most members of the Lily Family, it is a perennial herb with a thickened root, in this case a bulb. The plant reaches 16 inches in height with leaves up to 12 inches long and one-quarter inch wide. The leaves arise from the bulb (the stem is leafless) and resemble blades of grass except for the white stripe down the center. There are five to 15 flowers in a loose cluster formed by branches at the top of the stem. Instead of differentiated sepals and petals, the flowers have six identical perianth segments which look like petals. These are nearly one inch long, white with a green band on the back and taper at their tips. There are six stamens arranged around the base of the ovary which matures into a reverse egg-shaped six-angled capsule. According to Weeks and Bullen, the flowers open only in the sun.

Star of Bethlehem is cultivated in North America and is said to be the hardiest member of the genus here (Sunset, 1967). Bailey (1949) distinguishes it from the five other species he gives by the perianth segments having the green stripe, the leaves to only one foot in length and the flower clusters flat-topped as opposed to elongate.

Weeks and Bullen (1964) made the essence by the boiling method. They do not say why they chose the boiling method. (*Orinithogalum,* from Greek *òrnis, òrnithos,* bird, and *gála,* milk, perhaps alluding to the color of the perianth segments; *umbellatum,* in the form of an *umbélla* or parasol, referring to the flat-topped flower clusters.)

VERVAIN, *Verbèna officinális* Linnaeus, for "those with fixed principles and ideas . . . they have a great wish to convert those around them to their own views of life" (Bach, 1933, p. 22). Verbena Family (Verbenaceae). Vervain. The references give no synonyms. Bach's Vervain is probably native to the Mediterranean region, but occurs also in North Africa, in Asia east to the Himalayas and as an introduction in North America. It is reported as a weed of waste places in Amador and Trinity Counties in rural Northern California (Munz, 1959), suggesting that, although it is a plant which follows man around to a certain extent and is connected with human culture, as Hegi (1927, 5:3, p. 2240) says, it may not be able to tolerate our big cities as a number of European weeds are able to do. It is cultivated in North America, though evidently not frequently.

V. officinalis is a perennial herb with a woody root and several tough erect stems to two feet in height. The stems are square in cross section, branched above and clad with stiff hairs. The leaves, which are divided into fairly deep lobes, are one to three inches long, lance or diamond shaped, dull green and hairy like the stems. The lilac colored flowers are slightly more than one-eighth inch in diameter with a tubular lower portion and five spreading lobes and are without stalks in elongate clusters (spikes) at the ends of the branches. The fruit consists of four small reddish brown nutlets, like the fruits of the Mint Family (Lamiaceae, which also have four-angled stems), except that the *Verbena* nutlets have one well-defined face covered with tiny tubercles, or, in the case of Bach's species, with granules.

Weeks and Bullen (1964) specify that whole spikes should be gathered for making the essence. These should, they say, be taken from above dead or fading flowers but should not include too many unopened flowers. They prepared the essence by the sun method. (*Verbena*, classical Latin name for sacred boughs, as of laurel, myrtle or olive; *officinalis*, belonging to the herb store or pharmacy, *officìna*.)

WATER VIOLET, *Hottònia palústris* Linnaeus, for those "very independent, capable and self-reliant" individuals who "are aloof, leave people alone and go their own way" (Bach, 1933, p. 16). Primrose Family (Primulaceae). Water Violet. Synonym: *H. millefòlium* Gilibert. Bach's Water Violet is native in ponds and ditches of Central and Northern Europe east to Siberia according to FB, although FE places it no further east than Romania. In the British Isles it is rare except in parts of Scotland and Ireland. It is not generally mentioned in American horticultural references, though it should not be difficult to raise here as a pond subject, even in cold climates such as New England.

Water Violet is a floating fresh water aquatic perennial with whorled dissected leaves which grow below the water, stabilizing a stem which rises 1½ feet above the water. The flowers are in whorls at the top of the stem with a whorl of leaf-like bracts some distance beneath them. The green calyx is 1½ inches long and is divided almost to the base into more or less linear lobes. The one inch diameter corollas have five lilac colored lobes spreading at a right angle from the short tubular portion which is yellow at the throat (Weeks and Bullen describe the flowers as having a yellow "eye"). There are five stamens included within the corolla. The fruit is a round, five-valved capsule (a dry fruit which opens to release its seeds along definite lines of rupture) about one-quarter inch in diameter.

There is only one other *Hottonia* species, *H. inflàta* Elliott, Featherfoil, which is native near the east coast of the

VERVAIN *Verbena officinalis*

U.S. from Maine to Florida, west to Mississippi then north to Indiana and is also in West Virginia (Gleason, 1952). It grows in habitats similar to those of *H. palustris*. I believe it would make nearly as effective a Water Violet essence.

Weeks and Bullen (1964) specify the sun method for making this essence. Their technique for gathering flowers growing out in the water is quaint and agreeable: "It is useful to have a walking stick with a crooked handle to draw the plants gently to the bank as they often grow well out in the stream." (*Hottonia*, in honor of Peter Hotton, 1648–1709, professor of botany at Leiden, Holland; *palustris*, of the marsh, *pàlus*.)

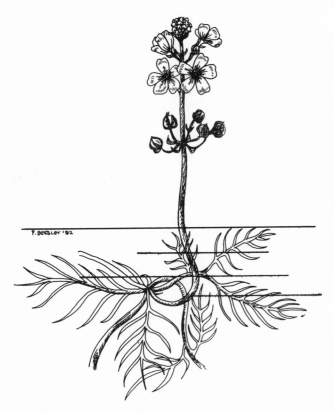

WATER VIOLET *Hottonia palustris*

WILD OAT, *Brómus ramòsus* Hudson, for those whose "difficulty is to determine what occupation to follow; as although their ambitions are strong, they have no calling which appeals to them above all others" (Bach, 1933, p. 12). Grass Family (Poaceae). Hairy Brome, Wood Brome, Wild Oat as used in connection with the flower essence. Synonyms: *B. altíssimus* Web. (Weber?), but not *B. altissimus* Gilibert nor *B. altissimus* Pursh; *B. ásper* Murray; *B. montànus* Scopoli; *B. nemoròsus* Villars; *Zérna ramosa* (Hudson) Lindman.

This is the only member of the Grass Family which Dr. Bach incorporated into his system. The grasses include the

cereal grains like wheat, oats, rye, barley and millet and other useful plants like bamboo and the various durable species that are planted as lawns. They are monocotyledons (see under Star of Bethlehem) and are generally accepted as highly evolved in that group. Their flowers, like those of the oaks and other evolutionarily reduced plants, can be difficult to recognize as flowers until they are examined closely and are seen to have all the essential parts. Lawrence (1951) puts it this way: ". . . the grass flower is a highly developed structure whose morphology is complicated by the extensive suppression of parts and reduction of the conventional floral elements." The way the flowers are grouped together into distinctive clusters called spikelets also has practically no parallel among the other plants, even among other wind-pollinated ones like the oaks. The generalized structure of a grass floret is shown in the sketch.

Wild Oat is native over most of Europe and is in North Africa and temperate Asia. It was thought for a time that it was present as an introduction in New England, but Fernald (1930) made a strong case that it was not by directly comparing the American plant with published descriptions and with a representative collection of *B. ramosus* from Europe and by identifying the New England suspect as a form of a native American species. A. S. Hitchcock (1950) gives *B. ramosus* as introduced into Washington state, but

---

Generalized cluster of grass flowers (spikelet) and individual flower (floret). Redrawn from Munz, 1959.

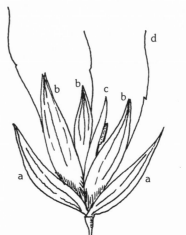
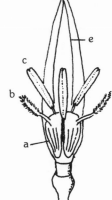

Grass spikelet:

a—glume
b—lemma
c—palea exposing a pair of anthers
d—awn

Floret with lemma removed:

a—ovary
b—style with feathery stigma
c—anther or pollen sac
d—palea with membranous margins
e—verse of palea

Flora of the Pacific Northwest (C. L. Hitchcock and Cronquist, 1973) indicates that this report also was based on a misidentification of an American species similar to *B. ramosus.*

B. ramosus is a perennial herb to five feet or even more in height. The leaves are the typical strap-shaped blades of grass, in this case a little more than half an inch wide, thinly hairy and rough to the touch. Where the blades clasp the stem they are clothed with long downward pointing hairs. The flower clusters (spikelets) are on long stalks which nod to one side of the stem. Each 1½ inch long spikelet contains a number of closely packed flowers (florets) above two abbreviated leaf- or bract-like structures called glumes. The lower glume is up to a quarter inch long, awl shaped with one nerve or fine rib running down its back. The upper glume approaches one-half inch in length, is lance-shaped and has three nerves. Each floret has an outer "petal" called a lemma, much like the upper glume, except that it is a little longer, has seven nerves and a slender flexible one-third inch long projection from its tip called an awn. There is a smaller thin membranous inner "petal" called a palea with two finely hairy green nerves on its backside. The anthers (pollen sacs) are between an eighth and a quarter inch long, rather long for a *Bromus* species, and at flowering time hang out of the floret on their slender filaments to be shaken by the wind, which disperses the pollen. The slender three-eighths inch long seed or grain is hairy at the tip and dark brown in color when mature.

Brome grasses are seldom cultivated as garden subjects, although a number of them are sown in pastures as forage for cattle. Some of the introduced European forage species have become widespread weeds in North America in both the city and the country (Crampton, 1974). Dr. Bach's species is not one of these. It could, of course, be cultivated. It comes close morphologically to some of our native perennial bromes, especially to *B. vulgaris* (Hooker) Shear, with which it was confused in the State of Washington and which is widespread in many plant communities in California, and also to the European *B. erectus* Hudson, which is sparingly naturalized in the U.S.

It is unclear how the name "oat" became associated with this plant in Dr. Bach's usage. *Oat* is almost always used to refer to the genus *Avena,* a quite different grass. However, *Bromus* is a Latinization of the classical Greek word for "oat." In any case, the name is now thoroughly established in connection with the flower essences. (*Bromus,* from Greek *brómos,* oats; *ramosus,* branching, from *ràmus,* branch.)

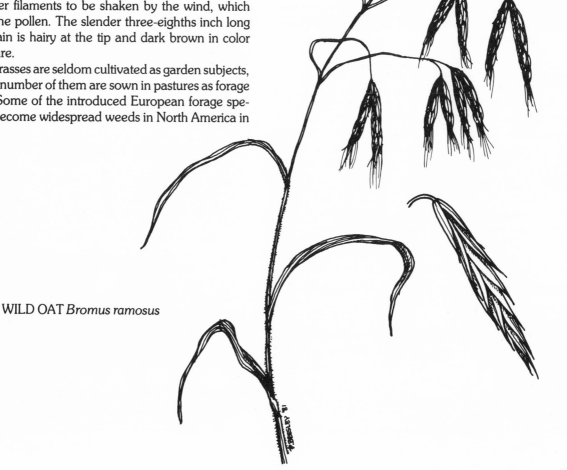

WILD OAT *Bromus ramosus*

Concluding Remarks

An overview of the botany of the Bach flowers shows that of the 36 species Dr. Bach chose for his essences, all but two are either native, naturalized or cultivated on at least two continents. More significantly, most of them occur as introductions or in cultivation on other continents also. The two that are restricted to Europe, Water Violet and Wild Oat, would be widespread there. Furthermore, almost all the Bach species are easy to cultivate in any temperate climate. Weeks and Bullen (1964) do say that "cultivated garden plants should never be used" for making essences, but I feel that if conditions are right, garden plants are acceptable for essences. (This would be consistent with Dr. Bach's making the Cerato essence from a garden shrub.) The garden should be located away from air pollution, a place where toxic pesticides and fertilizers are not used and, most of all, it should be a manifestation of love. (A future article in the *Flower Essence Journal* will deal with cultivation of Bach species.)

Thus these flower essence species, by their ecology and widespread distribution as well as in other respects, constitute Dr. Bach's "simple and natural method . . . for the lay healer and the home," (Bach, 1933), non-exclusive and accessible to all. It is my opinion that anyone with access to these plants in the many places where they grow can prepare essences from them and find that the essences will have the properties that Dr. Bach attributed to them.

Editor's note: It is the position of the Bach Centre that the flower essence properties described by Dr. Bach can only be properly applied to essences prepared from the same plant species in the same (mostly English) habitats used by Dr. Bach in the 1930's. While we feel that this is an unduly restrictive approach, it is true that any definitive statement about equivalence with Bach essences awaits further research and experience.

Addendum and Erratum.

I restudied all of the Bach species in the second edition (1962) of *Flora of the British Isles* when it became available to me this year, and also in *A New Illustrated British Flora* (Butcher, 1961) and found practically no information for any of them not contained in the first edition of FB or in FE.

In the third edition of the *Flower Essence Quarterly* (Autumn, 1980) there was an error in the bibliography in the citing of Hegi's *Illustrierte Flora von Mittel-Europa.* Hanser is the publisher of the second edition only, not both editions as the citation indicates. Lehmann published the entire first edition.

References

Abrams, L. R. *Illustrated Flora of the Pacific States.* Stanford: Stanford University Press, v. 3, 1951.

Bach, Edward. *The Twelve Healers and Other Remedies.* London: C. W. Daniel Co., Ltd., 1933, 1977.

Bailey, Liberty H. *Manual of Cultivated Plants Most Commonly Grown in the Continental United States and Canada.* New York: MacMillan Co., 1949.

Butcher, R. W. *A New Illustrated British Flora.* London: Leonard Hill, 1961.

Clapham, A. R., T. G. Tutin and E. F. Warburg. *Flora of the British Isles,* 2nd ed. (FB). Cambridge: Cambridge University Press, 1962.

Clark, David E., ed. *Sunset Western Garden Book.* Menlo Park: Lane Publishing Co., 1967.

Crampton, Beecher. *Grasses in California.* Berkeley: University of California Press, 1974.

Fernald, M. L. *Forms of American Gentians.* Rhodora, 19, 149, 1917.

————. *The Complex* Bromus ciliatus. Rhodora, 32, 70–71, 1932.

Gleason, H. A. *The New Britton and Brown Illustrated Flora of the Northeastern United States and Adjacent Canada.* Lancaster, Pa.: Lancaster Press, v. 3, 1952.

Hegi, Gustav. *Illustrierte Flora von Mittel-Europa.* München: J. F. Lehmanns Verlag, Bd. 1, 1908; 2, 1909; 3, 1912; 4:1, 1917; 4:2, 1923; 5:1, 1925; 5:3, 1927; 6:1, 1928; 6:2, 1929; 7, 1931.

Hitchcock, A. S. *Manual of the Grasses of the United States,* 2nd ed. New York: Dover Publications, vols. 1 and 2, 1971.

Hitchcock, C. L. and A. Cronquist. *Flora of the Pacific Northwest.* Seattle: University of Washington Press, 1973.

Howell, J. T. *Marin Flora, Manual of the Flowering Plants and Ferns of Marin County, California,* 2nd ed. with Supplement. Berkeley: University of California Press, 1970.

Lawrence, G. H. M. *Taxonomy of Vascular Plants.* New York: MacMillan Co., 1951.

Lewis, C. T. and C. Short. *A Latin Dictionary.* Oxford: The Clarendon Press, 1879.

Liddell, H. G. and R. Scott. *A Greek-English Lexicon,* 9th ed. Oxford: The Clarendon Press, 1940.

Munz, P. A. *A California Flora.* Berkeley: University of California Press, 1959, 1970.

Rehder, A. *Synopsis of the Genus* Lonicera. Annual Report of the Missouri Botanical Garden, 14, 27–232, 1903.

Stearn, W. T. *Botanical Latin,* 2nd ed. Newton Abbott (Great Britain): David and Charles, Ltd., 1973.

Tutin, T. G. et al. *Flora Europaea* (FE). Cambridge: Cambridge University Press, v. 1, 1964; 2, 1968; 3, 1972; 4, 1976; 5, 1980.

Weeks, Nora and Victor Bullen. *The Bach Flower Remedies, Illustrations and Methods of Preparation.* London: C. W. Daniel Co., Ltd., 1964.

David Siegler

Darrell Wright leading a flower walk for the Flower Essence Society.

EXPLORING CALIFORNIA FLOWER ESSENCES: PART IV, CONCLUSION

by Richard Katz

Early in 1980 the FES released to the public 24 new flower essences prepared in California from wildflowers and garden flowers. In previous issues of this journal, 12 of these essences have been described: six native wildflowers—California Poppy, Iris, Madia, Penstemon, Star Tulip and Yarrow; two naturalized wildflowers—wild Chamomile (Mayweed) and Scotch Broom; and four garden flowers—Borage, Fuchsia, Pink Yarrow and Sunflower. In this issue the remaining 12 essences in the set are described: five native wildflowers — Blackberry, Manzanita, Sagebrush, Scarlet Monkeyflower and Sticky Monkeyflower; three naturalized wildflowers — Red Clover, Self-Heal and wild Sweet Pea; and four garden flowers — Dill, Morning Glory, Nasturtium and Shasta Daisy. The article concludes with a discussion of our responsibilities as practitioners working with these new essences. — Ed.

David Siegler

BLACKBERRY *Rubus ursinus*

Blackberry

The wild Blackberry is widespread at lower elevations of the Pacific coast of North America from Southern California to British Columbia. A member of the Rose Family (Rosaceae), its leaves are composed of three leaflets, its flowers are white and five-petaled, and its berries ripen from bright red to shiny black. Blackberry brambles grow in thorny, trailing vines from three to six feet in height. The FES essence was first prepared from the species *Rubus ursinus* (also known as *R. vitifolius*) along the banks of Deer Creek near Nevada City, California.

Like the Scotch Broom, this plant is so prolific that it is considered by gardeners in many areas to be an invasive pest. Yet, like the Scotch Broom, the Blackberry bramble has a quality which can be quite valuable to us (besides the medicinal leaves and tasty berries). Applied to the subtle vibrational realm of essences, the Blackberry's quality of flourishing physical growth becomes the creative power of thought. It works with the principle that energy follows thought, that "as we think, so we become."

The abundant growth of the Blackberry can become a tangled mess if it is not consciously directed. Similarly, a jumble of contradictory thoughts can produce lives that are jumbled and ineffective. The lesson of the Blackberry essence is to become more aware of the process by which our thoughts are creating our reality, and to direct these thoughts in more conscious ways. It helps us to connect more deeply with our inner guidance, or higher self, and to use that connection to manifest more effectively in the physical world. Blackberry thus helps us to bridge from the more abstract to the more concrete levels of mind.

Blackberry essence works as a catalyst for taking appropriate action, helping us to clear away mental confusion and inertia which is separating us from the fulfillment of our goals. For example, one practitioner used it to break through her resistance to organizing her office. Another woman took Blackberry as part of a combination when she felt frustrated in her travel plans due to lack of money. She then went out and got a job and earned the money for her airplane fare. The same course of action had been available to her before she had taken the essence, but the Blackberry helped her change the mental attitude that had blocked her from acting on that possibility.

Blackberry has also been used as part of a "manifestation formula" along with Madia and Shasta Daisy. In this combination the Blackberry seems to provide the motivating creative energy, while Madia and Shasta Daisy act to focus and direct the way it is expressed. This essence is especially suited to use along with creative visualization, affirmation, active meditation and conscious dreaming. Its basic effect is to help raise our level of vibration so that the spiritual self be expressed more directly through our thoughts and actions, enabling us to more actively manifest our life purpose.

Manzanita

Manzanita is common to the mountainous regions of western North America, and ranges from a low groundcover to a small tree. The FES essence was prepared from the White-Leaf Manzanita, *Arctostaphylos viscida,* one of the species prevalent in the western foothills of California's Sierra Nevada mountains. This species grows from four to twelve feet high and, as most Manzanita species, it has twisted branches with dark-brown peeling bark (somewhat like its relative, the Madrone tree), with whitish-green oval leaves. The Manzanita blossoms are white to pinkish-white, sticky, bell-shaped and about one-half inch in length. They appear in late winter and early spring, and later ripen into small red berries, from which the Spanish name "manzanita," meaning "little apple," derives.

When I first prepared the essence in the Chicago Park area of Nevada County, California, the rugged, leathery branches, many of them closely hugging the ground, suggested the quality of grounding, of establishing a solid relationship with the physical earth and earthly things. At the same time, the delicate and sweet pinkish flowers suggested qualities of appreciation and affinity. Entering into a meditative attunement with the plant, I felt that these qualities in the essence might help people who do not fully accept their incarnation into physical form, who need to realize that the physical body and physical world are the dynamic expressions of spiritual energy in a "denser" form. The Manzanita, which often flourishes in rugged areas where few other plants grow, can teach us to accept and give life to physical reality, even if it is a difficult and challenging reality for us. It can help us to live and work effectively in the "waking consciousness" of the ordinary world, while retaining our connection to spiritual reality. Thus, Manzanita is one of the FES essences which specifically assists people opening to greater spiritual awareness to do so with more balance and grounding.

Manzanita has some similarity to the Bach essence Clematis, which is for the dreamy or mystical person who tends to leave the here-and-now for more pleasant escapes into fantasy and other realms. However, Manzanita

is more for the person who feels somehow "corrupted" by having to carry around a "gross" physical body in a "fallen" physical world. This attitude may express itself overtly as a path of renunciation and asceticism. More commonly, the attitude is unconsciousness, and is manifest as ambivalence toward the body and the physicality of the world, and sometimes as emotional extremes.

The following experience illustrates the typical use of the Manzanita essence. A woman I met on a cross-country ski outing near Nevada City, California, in late winter came to me for a selection of flower essences. She had been suffering for a number of years from a variety of physical ailments, which had only partially responded to allopathic and homeopathic treatments. In the course of our conversation, she revealed that her living habits were subject to extreme swings. Sometimes she would go for days with very little food or sleep, feeling very meditative and spiritual. Then she would go on a sleep/food binge for several days, seemingly unconscious, feeling very guilty and unspiritual.

Apparently this woman associated her spirituality with an almost disembodied state, and when her long-neglected physical needs asserted themselves, she could only respond to them by splitting off from her higher faculties. Radiesthesia and intuition indicated the Manzanita essence for her. When I described its qualities to her, she volunteered the insight that an underlying cause of her chronic physical complaints was her non-acceptance of being in her body. She also remembered that during the ski outing she had been surrounded by Manzanita shrubs beginning to blossom, and had felt a very stabilizing effect from them. Manzanita was teaching her the lesson that rather than being felt as a source of unspiritual corruption, the body could truly be experienced as the "temple of the spirit."

Local Color Photo

MANZANITA *Arctostaphylos viscida*

Sagebrush

Sagebrush (not to be confused with garden Sage—*Salvia* spp. of the Mint Family) belongs to the *Artemisia* genus, named for the Greek moon goddess Artemis. Other *Artemisia* species include Mugwort and Wormwood, and the genus has a reputation for dreamlike and magical properties. Sagebrush is a shrub, generally one to two feet in height, and like Mugwort and Wormwood it has grey-green leaves and is quite aromatic. European settlers to North America gave it the name "Sage" because its smell reminded them of the familiar *Salvia*. The species name— *A. tridentata*—refers to the "three teeth" of the Sagebrush's narrow leaves. The flowers appear in late summer or early autumn as small tufts of yellow at the end of the branches. Sagebrush is found in abundance in the high desert of the great Basin of the Western United States, including most of Nevada (where it is the state flower) and extending into eastern California. The FES essence was first prepared about ten miles east of Truckee, California, on the eastern side of the Sierra Nevada mountains.

Sagebrush has been well known for many healing properties by the Native American peoples living in the areas where it grows. Its uses, which primarily employ the leaves, range from external applications for wounds and rashes, to "smoking" a room or other environment to purify its energies (much as frankincense is traditionally used).

The qualities of the Sagebrush essence are related to the plant's use for purification. The essence helps us to let go of "excess baggage" from our personality, and shed layers of habits and self-images which obscure our essential being. Sagebrush may be used for major life cycles of purification (such as the "Saturn cycle" described in astrology) in which we make significant changes in identity. It can also be used for shorter or more temporary experiences, such as when we have absorbed the energy of another person or environment, and wish to clear it from ourselves. One actor reports using Sagebrush essence, in combination with Morning Glory, to clear way the "cobwebs" of a busy day working in the city, and to be able to contact the emotions at the depth of his being. Others report Sagebrush helpful when they are overly influenced by the praise of others, or the desire to make a good impression. The essence helps them to separate themselves from any expectations they have absorbed from others.

While there are some similarities between Sagebrush, the FES Yarrow essence and the Bach Walnut essences, there are important differences as well. Yarrow has a more protective or preventative quality, helping us become less vulnerable to disharmonious energies around us. Sagebrush, by contrast, is used more to eliminate energies we have already absorbed. The Bach Walnut, while it also

SAGEBRUSH *Artemisia tridentata*

enlargement of flower

helps free us of external influence, is primarily a strengthener, helping us to make important transitions and stay true to our soul's path. Sagebrush acts as a cleanser of the dross of accumulated conditioning, helping us cut through inessentials to reach the spiritual core of being.

Several women reported that their use of Sagebrush helped them to face deep emotions they had been avoiding and deal openly with these feelings. Another woman reported using Sagebrush at a time of major transition in her life, when she needed to let go of many attachments to past images of herself. She spent a lot of time in the desert environment of the Sagebrush, and felt its effect as stripping away all her masks and false personas, until she felt quite spiritually "naked."

Scarlet Monkeyflower

Scarlet Monkeyflower, *Mimulus cardinalis,* is botanically quite similar to the Common or Yellow Monkeyflower, *M. guttatus,* which is Dr. Bach's Mimulus. Both are herbaceous perennials growing in moist areas, such as along streams and in wet meadows. They each (along with Sticky Monkeyflower, whose description follows) have flowers with an upper lip of two petals and a lower lip of three petals, which is characteristic of the Snapdragon/Figwort Family (Scrophulariaceae) to which they belong.

Nonetheless, there are important differences between the Scarlet and the Common Monkeyflower, the most noticeable of which is the brilliant red of the *M. cardinalis* flowers, in contrast to the yellow flowers with red spots of *M. guttatus*. Scarlet Monkeyflower is also less common than the Yellow Monkeyflower, and it tends to bloom somewhat later in the year (mid- to late-summer, rather than spring to mid-summer). The FES essence was first prepared along a small stream in the North San Juan Ridge area of Nevada County, California.

Like Bach's Mimulus, Scarlet Monkeyflower essence deals with specific fears and conflicts, but it differs in its emphasis and in the quality of the fears with which it works. As its red color suggests, Scarlet Monkeyflower is for fear of emotions which express vital energy, particularly the "Mars-like" emotions of anger and aggression. It helps people who repress these emotions out of fear of

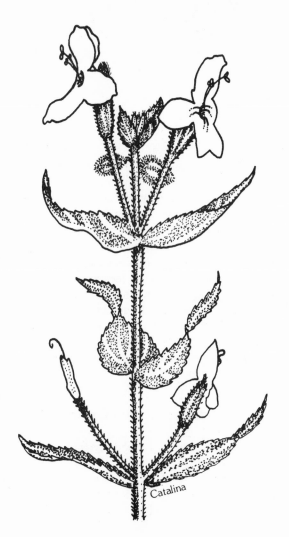

SCARLET MONKEYFLOWER *Mimulus cardinalis*

losing control or of social disapproval, or who are alienated from the "shadow side" of their personalities.

Scarlet Monkeyflower is often indicated for people who seem very tense, or who have little apparent vitality, and who seem fearful of expressing any emotion. Counseling, meditation and/or other means of enhancing self-awareness can help such people to contact buried feelings such as anger and resentment. In these cases, Scarlet Monkeyflower may be used to allay fears of working with these intense emotions. If an "awareness crisis" occurs, such as old angers "bubbling up" into awareness, this can be handled with the help of a counselor or friend, and/or by meditation and self-observation. The goal is to unblock the life energy that is tied up in the repressed anger and in the fear of the anger, so that it can be transformed into appropriate expressions of healthy self-assertion and enthusiastic participation in life.

Awareness of emotions can be developed with a sense of detachment and non-identification. One woman using Scarlet Monkeyflower commented that "emotions came up, but I had an unemotional perspective on them, so it was easier to release and change the situation." Another way that these emotions can be processed is through the dream state.

A key factor in successful transmutation of negative emotions is the ability to accept ourselves and the fact that we are experiencing the emotions. Thus, practitioners have found the Self-Heal essence (described later in this article) to be a good balancer and stabilizer in many cases when used along with Scarlet Monkeyflower. (It has a similar use with Fuchsia essence.) It should be pointed out, however, that acceptance of emotions is not the same as giving license to the free expression of negativity (one of the misunderstandings of the "encounter group movement" of the sixties). The unique quality of flower essences is that they give us the possibility of working with powerful emotions in a more subtle and inner way.

Observations from some practitioners using Scarlet Monkeyflower have further clarified its use. One distinguished between the Fuchsia essence, which unblocks emotions associated primarily with the heart-center, and the Scarlet Monkeyflower, which works more with solar-plexus-center emotions. This observation is corroborated by another practitioner who noted that this essence is particularly indicated for individuals who resent the power of others. (Power is associated with the solar-plexus center.)

The true lesson of the Scarlet Monkeyflower is the reconciliation of the opposites of our personality. It is a tool for releasing the vitality and free-flowing positive feeling which is "banished" with the repressed negativity or the "shadow" parts of our personality. Its goal is to bring our emotional energy into full harmony with the light, clarity and wisdom of our highest conscious understanding and compassion for self and others.

Sticky Monkeyflower

Sticky Monkeyflower, also known as Orange Bush Mimulus, is a perennial shrub about one to four feet in height, which grows abundantly along the hillsides of California. The FES essence was first prepared from the species *Mimulus aurantiacus,* which is found especially in the coastal ranges of northern and central California. Sticky Monkeyflower differs from both the Common Monkeyflower (*M. guttatus*) and the Scarlet Monkeyflower (*M. cardinalis*) in that it is a woody perennial shrub which grows on drier hillsides, whereas the other species are herbaceous plants growing in moist meadows and along streams. *M. aurantiacus* flowers are orange-colored, and not spotted as the *M. guttatus* flowers, and its leaves, unlike the bright green of the herbaceous species, are dark green above, grey-green below and sticky (hence the common name). The differences are distinct enough that some botanists classify Sticky Monkeyflower in a separate genus *Diplacus,* rather than in *Mimulus.*

This essence was among the first that I prepared in California, and it gave me an insight about the effect of botanical variations of similar plants upon the qualities of their essences. When I first encountered the Sticky Monkeyflower near Cazadero in Sonoma County, California, I felt extremely attracted to it, yet puzzled by its differences from Bach's Mimulus, which I knew to be the essence for specific fears and worries. I prepared the Sticky Monkeyflower essence, meditated and attuned to its energy, and considered if there might be some fear or conflict of mine to which it related. With the help of a friend, I realized that I had been experiencing much conflict concerning sexual energy and intimacy. I was at a large gathering at the time, and was feeling an old awkwardness about social situations that reminded me of my worst moments of adolescence. It seemed that I was attracted to this flower, then, because it was working with the specific fear/conflict about sexuality and its relationship to other aspects of my life: intimacy with others and the flow of my creative and vital energies.

I began sharing this essence with some associates and friends to see if my perceptions were accurate, or might simply be a projection of my own immediate mood and feelings (an important distinction for this work). I found that the essence was repeatedly indicated (through counseling and radiesthesia) for individuals for whom sexuality was an issue. However, I found that the particular way the sexual issue presented itself to these people showed considerable variation. For some it was a case of the need to break free of classical patterns of repression. For others it was the "opposite" situation, the need to balance out an over-obsession with sex. Many people found their sexual energy blocked by emotional fears of intimacy related to past hurts and rejections, and others were confused about

their sexual orientation. For a few the sexual issue was more implicit, manifesting as a general blockage of the life force, or of creativity.

In each case the Sticky Monkeyflower helped bring the concerns about sexuality and intimacy into greater focus, with more clarity and willingness to work openly with these issues. It helped these people to integrate sexuality or related energies into the overall balance of their lives (often with other essences used in combination or sequence).

For example, this essence was used successfully by a woman who had developed her self-awareness through many years of spiritual and inner-growth practices, and was aware that her fears about sexuality and intimacy were hindering her spiritual development. She used Sticky Monkeyflower as part of an essence combination, and was able to let go of feelings of anger and hurt which had been blocking intimate relations with a man she loved. The feelings dated back to a rape incident when she was a girl of five, and through her use of the essences she was able to

STICKY MONKEYFLOWER *Mimulus aurantiacus*

become more accepting of her body and to overcome her fear of intimacy.

Another woman who had completely closed down her sexual feelings for a period of more than four years after having been rejected in a relationship, reported that after taking Sticky Monkeyflower she began dreaming of her former lovers, and gradually became more aware of her sexual energy.

Another use of Sticky Monkeyflower is exemplified by a man who was obsessively concerned about his sexual performance, and with finding new sexual partners. After using the essence for several weeks he reported that he was surprised to find himself less preoccupied with sex, and becoming more interested in developing friendships with women. He had not lost his sexual drive, but his attention had shifted to opening up his heart feelings. Later, he did become interested in a sexual relationship with a woman with whom he felt a strong bond of love, which was a new experience for him.

Practitioners report that Sticky Monkeyflower also works effectively in combinations of essences. For example, a major wholistic medical clinic uses a combination of Sticky Monkeyflower, Scarlet Monkeyflower and Yarrow with many of their patients who are starting with flower essences, and who need to deal with relationship problems. A flower essence practitioner in New Zealand reports that she uses a combination of Sticky Monkeyflower with the Bach essences Holly and Red Chestnut as a formula for developing unconditional love.

It is important for practitioners working with this essence to realize that for many people in our culture the sexual issue is quite volatile, and can generate highly charged feelings. If a client seems likely to over-react upon being told that an essence is working with sexuality, it may be advisable to allow the person to first experience the balancing effects of the essence before explicitly discussing sexuality. In any case, a skillful practitioner will work with the sexual issue in the context of the client's openness to intimacy, ability to love, and acceptance of his or her vitality and creative drive. Sexual energy becomes an object of fear, conflict or obsession when it is experienced as something *separate* from us; the goal of working with flower essences is to *integrate* sexuality with the balance of our lives.

For this reason, it would be a mistake to regard Sticky Monkeyflower as some kind of "sex potion," or to encourage the expectation that it will be a sexual stimulant or aphrodisiac (which it is not). It is conceivable that this misinterpretation could in itself be experienced as sexually stimulating. (As Jeanne Rose says in *Herbs & Things,* "The most powerful of all aphrodisiacs is your brain.") However, this would be more in the nature of an acting out of unconscious projections and desires, rather than any effect of the essence itself.

As reported by numerous practitioners, Sticky Monkeyflower is an effective essence for balancing sexual and related energies. For some people, the effect of the essences is not explicitly sexual, but rather deals with a freeing of creative energy which can be considered a "higher octave" of sexual energy. Other FES essences (not included in this first set of 24) have also proven helpful in working with specific aspects of sexual and related energies. However, the Sticky Monkeyflower remains the most general FES essence for bringing these issues into awareness, for it works with the basic fears which must be mastered before any more specific sexual issues can be faced.

In summary, the effect of Sticky Monkeyflower essence is to lead a person from a state of fear, conflict or confusion about sexuality and intimacy, to a state in which the sexual impulse is fully integrated with physical vitality, heart-felt love, creative inspiration and spiritual attunement. This image of total sexual integration may seem to be an ideal beyond our reach. Yet, it is a vision which can inspire and challenge us to transcend millennia of cultural conditioning.

The "sexual revolution" of recent decades has brought sexuality openly into our awareness. More recently has come the realization that obsession with sex is no more liberating that was repression. Yet we cannot return to the restrictions of past generations, nor impose the constraints of repressive religious traditions, without denying ourselves our full evolutionary potential. For it is our challenge in this age to consciously restore sexuality to its rightful place in human life, to know it as a sacred expression of divine purpose, as a metaphor and vehicle for unity and creation, as an affirmation of love and of the joy of life, and as one of many forms of expression of the life force.

Sticky Monkeyflower has thus been added to the repertory of flower essences because it represents a major lesson we need to master in this age: the marriage of sexuality and spirituality, and the penetration of the sense of sacredness into all aspects of our lives.

Red Clover

Red Clover was brought to North America from Europe, and planted extensively as a cover and forage crop. It has now become naturalized throughout the continent. Its familiar three leaflets are indicated by the genus name (first part) of its botanical name, *Trifolium pratense.* Red Clover is a highly medicinal herb, especially known for the tea made from its pinkish-red blossoms, which is an excellent blood-purifier. The FES essence was first prepared at the Oak Valley Herb Farm, about 25 miles from Nevada City, California, in the Sierra Nevada foothills.

As a flower essence, Red Clover acts to purify the aura or energy field of an individual from emotions of fear,

RED CLOVER
Trifolium pratense

panic and hysteria absorbed from others, especially from groups, or from mass consciousness. One practitioner reported it also helped work with the archetypal images of fear and panic associated with the collective unconscious.

Red Clover differs in emphasis from Pink Yarrow, which is for people who suffer from extreme psychic sensitivity, and who tend to identify with, or match the emotional moods of others, or who feel themselves to be the targets of such moods. Pink Yarrow, like Yarrow, is a "protective" essence, whereas Red Clover, like Sagebrush, is a "purifying" essence. However, while Sagebrush helps release wrong identifications and attachments, Red Clover is for releasing the rather hypnotic emotional states of hysteria, obsessive fear and panic.

A good illustration of Red Clover use occurred when an FES member attended a lecture about predictions of upcoming earth changes. He found that much of the audience was caught up in the "gloom-and-doom" attitude of the speaker, which was also beginning to affect him. At a break in the lecture he took some Red Clover essence, and

found that for the rest of the talk he was able to listen to and objectively evaluate the information presented, without being swept up in the negative emotions of those around him.

In another case, Red Clover was used with Penstemon by a woman caught in a natural disaster area of severe flooding and mud-slides along the California coast. She became quite distressed listening to radio news reports and absorbing the highly-charged negative emotions of those around her. She felt overwhelmed, and unable to release any feeling. After taking the essences she was able to cry, and then to find her inner peace. She finally relaxed and got some long-overdue sleep. She reported that the sense of inner peace was lasting.

Red Clover has also been reported to be useful in more personal situations, as exemplified by one woman who used it when going to visit her disapproving parents. Rather than being stifled with fear of their reactions, as in previous visits, she felt in touch with an inner sense of clarity, and more able to respond to her parents in a calm, loving way.

Red Clover is an invaluable tool for the coming years of upheaval, assisting us in maintaining clarity and calm amidst the personal upsets and mass reactive emotions which are all too pervasive in a society struggling with change. Examples of situations in which it would be helpful might include a non-violent demonstration threatened with police violence, panic-stricken crowds in a natural disaster, a medical relief center in a disaster or combat zone, a population subjected to war propaganda, or a group of people being incited by a hateful speaker. Thus, we recommend that along with the Bach Rescue Remedy, and the FES Yarrow essence, you include Red Clover essence in your "psychic first aid kit." Even if you are the only one who is physically taking the essence, you can project its calming, clearing vibration to others in a very powerful way.

Self-Heal

Self-Heal is another herbal "immigrant" to North America from Europe with a long lineage of healing uses, as attested by its common names "Self-Heal" and "Heal-All." An erect perennial four to twelve inches high, *Prunella vulgaris* has lancelote leaves topped with a spike of beautiful violet flowers. A member of the Mint Family (Lamiaceae), Self-Heal is found in moist meadows and slopes, as well as in many gardens and lawns, and it is now widely distributed throughout the Northern Hemisphere. The FES essence was first prepared in a meadow at the Oak Valley Herb Farm.

As an herb, Self-Heal is used both internally and externally, and it is noted for its astringent, carminative and diuretic properties. As a flower essence, it works in a general, but very powerful way to enhance our awareness of our own inner power of healing. (The name of the flower is the affirmation of the essence!) More than the application of any particular technique, or the administration of a specific remedy, what is required for healing to take place is the development of a *healing attitude,* an attitude of self-confidence, acceptance, trust and love that can unlock the mind-body's own innate healing powers. This is what shows up as the mysterious "placebo effect" in scientific tests. It is the healing power of the *belief* that healing is taking place, even if there is no physical healing agent being administered. This self-healing attitude is just as real as any physical remedy, and it is the function of the Self-Heal essence to enhance that latent capacity within us.

Self-Heal thus works well with other essences and health modalities, and is often used as a centering or balancing essence in combination with others, particularly with the more cathartic essences. By opening our hearts to greater self-love, the Self-Heal essence helps us relax more with our changes, helps us to more fully accept all aspects of ourselves, as we experience the often painful process of letting go of our suffering.

One practitioner reported that Self-Heal has encouraged self-love with people who feel that they "don't deserve to be here." Another reports that she uses Self-Heal with people who identify their emotional needs with external sources, for example, "I need my lover's presence." The essence helps people find emotional nourishment within, as in the feeling, "I am complete. I have all I need."

Self-Heal essence is also quite effective when used as an adjunct to physical therapies, and can be added to salves, lotions and massage oils, much as the Bach Rescue Remedy or Crab Apple. It seems to work with the body of energy (etheric body) which is closest to the physical body, and thus can be a catalyst to a process of physical healing without itself having any direct physical effect. (In cases of actual physical disease, we recommend treatment by a qualified medical practitioner, whether or not flower essences are used.)

A typical example of such use of Self-Heal was as part of an essence combination given to a man who had been badly injured in a motorcycle accident. Self-Heal was included because the injuries, although being treated medically, were taking an excessively long time to heal. The man was experiencing so much anger about the accident, and thinking about it so obsessively, that he was neglecting to direct the necessary healing energy to his body. After about three weeks taking the essences internally, and applying Self-Heal externally, along with some acupressure sessions, the man reported his injuries much improved.

Another man used Self-Heal and Star of Bethlehem (a Bach essence for shock) both externally and internally

SELF-HEAL *Prunella vulgaris*

after having a severe reaction to an insect bite. The essences helped calm him down and allow his body's self-healing mechanisms to take care of the bite and swelling within a day.

A woman reported that she used Self-Heal after returning home from a strenuous trip. She felt exhausted, and physically and emotionally constipated. After using the essence for several days, she realized that the most caring thing she could do for her body would be to fast for several days, and to de-toxify. This feeling came from a deepened sense of self-acceptance and self-love, as the Self-Heal essence acted as a catalyst for her to feel the self-healing impulse within her.

Several sources have indicated that this essence may enhance the ability to receive nourishment directly from subtle energy, and thus it may be a good aid in programs of fasting. Another indicated use is as an adjunct to programs of visualization and affirmation used with people with chronic diseases. Again, the Self-Heal essence is not in itself a treatment for the condition, but its function is to open the inner reservoir of healthy self-love and acceptance which is the source out of which true healing flows.

Sweet Pea

This wild Sweet Pea, also know as Everlasting Pea *(Lathyrus latifolus),* is just as beautiful as the garden Sweet Pea *(Lathyrus odoratus),* but it does not have the same sweet scent. Its deep red-purple flowers (occasionally white) rise from long trailing vines throughout many roadsides and meadows of North America and its native Europe. The FES essence was first prepared along Deer Creek, near Nevada City, California.

The wild Sweet Pea has an interesting habit of clustering its growth around old inhabited settlements. The flower essence seems to be an expression of this "social" quality of the plant, as it helps people feel their rootedness in social relations, and to develop a natural sense of social responsibility (i.e., the ability to respond to others, rather than a sense of obligation to others).

One practitioner reported that Sweet Pea was useful in harmonizing relationships of couples. It enhanced the quality of being present with the other person, of listening with sincere attention and interest. Another practitioner has reported that the issue of "being present" was central to the ability to relate to others. The main obstacle in her "Sweet Pea" clients seemed to be "unfinished family business," that is, emotions and attitudes from childhood family experiences that had never been brought into full awareness and released. She found the Sweet Pea essence a valuable catalyst for completing such past cycles, and allowing people to be open to the social relations which are available to them in present time.

Sweet Pea essence has also proven helpful for such temporary experiences of social disorientation as return-ing home from a long trip, or being in conflict with family members or friends. One woman used it successfully when she was on the verge of leaving her family, which included several children. The flower essence enabled her to re-discover her underlying sense of relationship and belonging with her family that had been temporarily lost while in the throes of emotional conflict.

This essence is indicated, too, for people who have difficulty feeling at home in their communities, or who are seeking the right community to call home. It can help in the transition from the patterns of individualism associated with the Piscean Age, to the group-relational patterns which are emerging in the Aquarian Age. A specific application of Sweet Pea in this context would be for hermit- or monk-types of personalities who wish to participate more in society. Although somewhat similar to the Bach Water Violet essence in this respect, Sweet Pea is more for the person who needs to overcome fear, alienation or confusion about social relations, while Water Violet is for the very aloof person who feels "above" others.

Sweet Pea essence can also be used to enhance group process in therapy, study or work groups, or other meetings, and promises to be helpful in programs building healthy social relations in people manifesting anti-social behavior such as juvenile delinquency.

Dill

Dill is a familiar kitchen herb and European native in the Parsley/Carrot Family (Apaceae). It has soft, feathery leaves and an umbel (umbrella-like) flower head about six inches wide, with clusters of small yellow flowers. The FES essence was originally prepared from *Anethum graveolens* cultivated in the organic garden of the Oak Valley Herb Farm, and subsequently in other organic gardens. Dill herb and seed are not only known for their culinary uses, but they have carminative properties: they expel flatulence (intestinal gas). As with the Chamomile essence, Dill essence represents a "higher octave" of the physical properties of the herb. Flatulence is usually caused by poor digestion and assimilation of foods, often when many kinds of foods are mixed together, or are eaten too quickly. Working in the realm of vibrations, Dill essence deals with the digestion and assimilation of "psychic food"—our experiences. It helps us when we are reeling from an overload of stimulus, from too much happening too quickly.

This essence seems particularly appropriate for intense urban environments and high-stress lifestyles. One woman successfully used Dill when moving from a rural area to a high-pressured job in a large city. Suzanne Garden has developed a combination of Dill, Pink Yarrow and Yarrow, which she uses as a general-purpose balancer of energy.

SWEET PEA
Lathyrus latifolus

Catalina

DILL *Anethum graveolens*

Morning Glory

Morning Glory *(Ipomoea purpurea)* is a native of the tropical regions of the Americas, and is a garden favorite in North America and Europe, where it has escaped from cultivation in many areas. It is a climbing vine with heart-shaped leaves circling its stems, and with funnel-shaped blossoms. The FES essence was first prepared from the brilliant blue blossoms of the "Heavenly Blue" variety of Morning Glory at the Oak Valley Herb Farm.

In shamanistic traditions, the Morning Glory plant has been associated with visionary experiences. While the flower essence has no such effect, it does help people to view their lives from a fresh perspective. It is an essence which helps break up crystallized mental attitudes and behavior patterns. It also seems to work with the flow of the etheric counterpart of the nervous system, which seems to be related to the system of acupuncture meridians. Morning Glory essence is thus used with restlessness, jitteriness,

Dill is one of the more quickly acting of the FES flower essences. One woman reported that she took Dill at a time when her life was full of stressful changes: leaving a community, starting a relationship, confronting financial problems, living in crowded quarters. One night, after a stressful day in a workshop with 30 participants, this woman broke down in tears, feeling completely overwhelmed. She took some Dill essence and immediately "snapped out of it," feeling that she could now handle the situation.

Practitioners report that Dill is useful for many kinds of temporary stresses such as job pressures, interpersonal conflicts, final-exam week, overloaded appointment schedules, traveling, too much housework to do, or children making too much noise. After such situational use of Dill in a number of circumstances, one practitioner found that she was able to handle day-to-day stresses more easily, and needed to take the essence less and less.

Dill has also been helpful for people stuck in chronic patterns of feeling overwhelmed who consistently feel that life is "too much" to handle, and who seem to walk "shell-shocked" through the city streets. Such people tend to identify the source of their experience of overwhelm as "out there." Dill helps them to see, instead, that it is an inner attitude which creates the feeling of being overwhelmed. It transforms that feeling into a more detached perspective, which frees our mental processes to become more receptive to our inner knowing. It then becomes clear just how to handle the situations which had seemed so overbearing.

Thus, Dill's effect is to create a calmer, more centered state of being, and an enhanced ability to flow with the varied experience of life.

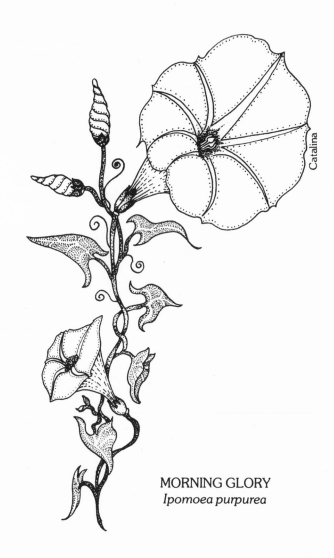

MORNING GLORY
Ipomoea purpurea

Steve Koke

hyperactivity and nervous habits. One woman took Morning Glory to get a fresh perspective on the seeming drudgery of her housework, and found that it not only lightened her attitude, but she stopped biting her nails for the first time in years. Some people have also found Morning Glory useful for insomnia, helping them to wake up in the morning feeling bright and refreshed. (Another flower name affirmation!)

Morning Glory can be used by people trying to break free of such ingrained habits as overeating or abuse of alcohol, coffee, sugar, cigarettes or drugs. Since such habits have many physiological aspects, as well as the psychological causes, they are most effectively treated by a multifaceted program of physical, psychological and spiritual therapies. In such a program, flower essences such as Morning Glory can be valuable catalysts which, by enhancing awareness and balancing the flow of vital energy, allow the person to respond more effectively to the various therapies in the treatment program.

It is important to support this use of Morning Glory with the conscious intent (will) of the individual to break the habit or addiction. Also important is self-awareness or a support system which can enable the person to deal with the underlying emotional conflicts that may be brought to the surface as the addictive avoidance patterns are given up. For this reason, Morning Glory is usually combined with other essences which correspond to the core emotions that need to be processed. (Some creative artists have reported that they specifically use Morning Glory to put them in touch with their deepest emotions.)

Morning Glory is essentially a *balancer* of vital energy, applicable to those experiencing erratic ups and downs (as in hypoglycemia) or extremes of high and low energy. When there is a smoother flow of vital energy, when habits and conditioning have less hold on us, then we can more readily contact the deeper aspects of ourselves. Thus, Morning Glory is an important essence for catalyzing deep inner change.

Nasturtium

The Nasturtium flower is also native to the tropical jungles of the Americas. Like the Fuchsia, it was imported into Europe, where it became a popular garden flower, and from there was introduced into cultivation in North America. It is mostly known to us today as a garden flower, although it has escaped from cultivation and naturalized in some California beach areas. It is a rapidly growing perennial (generally grown as an annual), with bright green shield-like leaves on long stalks growing from the vines. The flowers are of many colors, usually brilliant yellow, orange or red. Shaped with a spur in back, the flowers have distinct "honey-guide" markings inside the corollas to lead the bees to the nectar and pollen. Both the leaves and the flowers of the Nasturtium are eaten in salads, and have a strong peppery flavor. The flower was named for the Water Cress *(Nasturtium officinale),* because of the similar taste, and is known to the English as "Indian Cress." The FES essence was first prepared in the Ananda Community Garden near Nevada City, California, using the orange-colored blossoms of *Tropaeolum majus.*

As its brilliant colors suggest, *vitality* is the keynote of the Nasturtium. While preparing the essence I envisioned an earthy dancer, pulsating with life energy, yet poised and balanced with spiritual awareness. The essence has

NASTURTIUM *Tropaeolum majus*

helped people who are overly dry intellectually, and who are alienated from the circulation of life energy through their bodies and emotions. One woman using Nasturtium essence described it as "very earthy, just what my over-active intellect needed!" This would be a useful essence to bring more balance to people deeply involved in academic life, or in other lines of work in which left-brain analytic skills predominate.

Nasturtium has also proven useful for a temporary pick-up of energy, and has been used topically as an ingredient in stimulating massage oils and facial rinses. It is helpful when one feels run-down, whether due to an illness such as a cold, or to overwork, or simply because one is out of touch with one's body. Nasturtium is good for people who tend to be lethargic, and for those needing to awaken the energy in their lower chakras, to stimulate the *fire* within them. It is not a specific stimulant for any particular emotion or sensation associated with these chakras (energy centers), but rather is an overall catalyst for re-awakening the dormant life juices and vital energy which can animate our experience.

Both Manzanita and Nasturtium essences are applicable to people who need to be more in touch with their physical energy. While Manzanita deals with the issue of *acceptance* of physical experience, Nasturtium is more for *stimulating* our vitality. For example, a woman reported that she used Nasturtium when she started to feel run down after a long spell of tedious office work. She was feeling more and more de-vitalized, and realized that unless something changed she was risking coming down with a cold or flu. After using Nasturtium essence for several days, she reported that her body felt more "awake," and she took some time to get physical exercise, and to go to a sauna.

In summary, the lesson of the Nasturtium essence is to be vitally alive in all that we do, and to be aware of our physical energy as a necessary balance and grounding to the more subtle mental and spiritual energies.

SHASTA DAISY *Chrysanthemum maximum*

Shasta Daisy

Shasta Daisy is a hardy perennial garden flower, usually four to six feet in height, with large composite flower heads having yellow centers and white ray flowers ("petals"). It is a horticultural variety of *Chrysanthemum maximum,* a flower native to the Pyrenees region of Europe. The Shasta Daisy was developed in California by Luther Burbank and named for Mount Shasta. Although generally found in gardens, it has escaped cultivation in some areas of northern California. The FES essence was originally prepared at Oak Valley Herb Farm.

As with the Madia, which is also in the Composite/Sunflower Family (Asteraceae), Shasta Daisy works with the principle of integration and synthesis. The composite structure of the flower head, central disk flowers surrounded by ray flowers, is a living symbol of this synergistic principle. In fact, one writer reported that while using Shasta Daisy essence, an image came to him in meditation of a central circle uniting a number of other circles. This image, which was symbolic of the flower itself, gave him an insight about relating a number of concepts in a book he was writing. When used in conjunction with planning a project, organizing an office, or similar activities, the essence has the effect of helping the mind integrate information from a number of different sources, and organize it into a coherent whole. It is thus especially useful for students, writers, teachers, administrators, office workers and others doing work requiring mental organization.

For scattered seekers who are trying to decide what path in life to follow, and who collect information and ideas from many teachers and books, the Shasta Daisy helps bring a personal sense of integration. It assists us in weaving a whole fabric of understanding from the many diverse threads of information we have gathered. The essence teaches us that it is our own inner sense of self, our unique individuality which expresses our spiritual essence in life, which is the center from which we can integrate and synthesize the many inputs of information, attitudes, ideas and experiences which come to us. Rather than looking to choose from various external sources of meaning, we can find our sense of wholeness in our own center.

Shasta Daisy is often used effectively in combination with Madia, which strengthens the will and concentration in relation to mental activity. Shasta Daisy then helps "spiritualize" the intellect with the principle of unity, enabling us to see the whole forest and not just the individual trees. This essence is one of those especially helpful for self-actualization and fulfillment of life purpose. The Bach Wild Oat essence helps us contact the basic direction and purpose of our lives, while Shasta Daisy (usually with Madia) helps us to more specifically identify and focus upon that purpose and direction which is our own. With Blackberry added to the Shasta Daisy and Madia (the "manifestation formula"), it becomes a powerful catalyst for realizing that life purpose in specific, concrete action.

Concluding Comments

This article completes our series, "Exploring California Flower Essences," yet we have just begun our exploration of the gifts of the flower kingdom. Against the backdrop of herbal traditions of hundreds and thousands of years, the few years of experience with the FES essences, and even the 50 years of experience with the Bach essences, are clearly but initial chapters in the unfolding history of flower essences.

Thus, this first set of 24 FES essences is not intended to be an all-inclusive system, nor is it a replacement for the 38 Bach essences. Rather, it is an expansion of the existing repertory of flower essences, in response to the needs of the times, which enables practitioners to make a more precise selection of the most effective essences for an individual at any particular time. It is a step in the devel-

opment of a more universal understanding of flower essences, and an invitation for other practitioners and researchers of sufficient attunement to participate in this process of discovery.

Flower essence practitioners are thus encouraged to use their own intuitive and observational abilities to expand upon the general descriptions given for the FES essences. All essence descriptions should be considered as interpretations of universal energy applied to particular times, places, people and situations. They invariably reflect the limits of culture, experience, belief and language. Nevertheless, verbal guidelines can be valuable, and become more comprehensive as we add the cumulative insights of many practitioners. Even the Bach essences, in use for half a century, are still yielding new messages and interpretations as our experience and awareness grows.

". . . a balance of intuitive and analytic faculties . . ."

Our flower essence exploration also continues to expand as new essences are developed and released for research and use. While the essences described here were all prepared in California, our work is becoming more planetary with contributions of other regions of the world. *(See issue #3, pp. 36–37.)* Reports of insights, observations and case studies with new essences are a regular feature of the Flower Essence Society Members' Newsletter, as part of the Society's networking and research activities.

Participation in a communications network such as this is a responsibility requiring a high level of maturity and self-awareness. It requires a balance of intuitive and analytic faculties, of receptivity and discrimination, of openness and groundedness. It calls for the sharpness of penetrating insight, along with the gentleness of compassionate understanding. We need to know ourselves well enough to separate our projections from the real qualities of the essences, and to distinguish between our own needs and those of our clients. We must be knowing in our selection of essences, and skillful in our self-examination or counseling when navigating the sometimes rough waters of "awareness crises" or transformational upheavals. We should be confident in expressing what we know, yet humble in our willingness to learn from our mistakes and the feedback of others. Above all, we must not let petty fears, rivalries and ego needs obscure the spiritual service to which we are called.

Flower essences are an expression of the life-giving Spirit in Nature, which is always there for us to receive. If we are open to this gift, we can then serve the flourishing of that Spirit in all its forms.

A PERSPECTIVE ON THE BACH AND FES FLOWER ESSENCES

by Richard Katz

Plants have been used throughout history to enhance human health on both physical and spiritual levels. The herbal traditions of many cultures speak of the restorative capacities of flowers and the curative power of water (e.g., holy waters). Much of this knowledge has been lost or forgotten, or lies buried in the collective unconscious memory of humanity. It is the task of our age to bring such knowledge back into our conscious awareness, and to make it an integral part of our lives.

Dr. Bach was an English medical doctor, homeopath, spiritual initiate and healer, who developed a set of 38 flower essences in the 1930's. His life was guided by a deep sense of spiritual purpose and a desire to serve humanity. He was acutely sensitive to the spiritual causes of human suffering, and was finely attuned to the healing energies of Nature. Bach realized that disease is a sign of imbalance in one's emotions, attitudes and life directions, and that genuine well-being occurs only when one is true to one's spiritual essence and purpose.

Since Dr. Bach's death in 1936, the Bach remedies have been prepared by the Dr. Bach Centre in Sotwell, England. The Centre is located in a small house once used by Dr. Bach, where the remedies are prepared following Dr. Bach's methods, often using the same plant habitats as were used 50 years ago. Besides preparation and distribution of the Bach remedies, the Centre also publishes a newsletter and answers inquiries from around the world.

Inspired by my knowledge of Dr. Bach's work in England, I began preparing essences from California garden and wildflowers in 1978, applying preparation methods described in the Bach literature along with my own training in herbology and a number of meditative and spiritual disciplines. Motivated by a personal quest to experience and understand the healing source of the flower essences, I was also guided by a sense of urgent need for new tools of planetary healing in this age of transformation.

Initial experiences with the new essences I prepared in California (sometimes called the "California Flower Essences") were with a small group of practitioners and clients with whom I shared my discoveries. They indicated that these essences worked especially with processes of inner growth and spiritual awakening, serving as catalysts for the transmutation of specific blockages such as fears about sexuality, issues of intimacy, sensitivity, psychic and

spiritual development. In addition, I developed statements of affirmation for the new essences, as well as for the 38 Bach remedies, to emphasize their positive transformative qualities.

Numerous requests were received to make the new essences available, and to share my work openly with the public. Although the indications for the essences were still quite tentative, they were already proving their timeliness and value. I thus decided to release 24 of the new essences to the public in 1980, and at the same time to promote a communications network of flower essence practitioners, educators and researchers through the Flower Essence Society. A second set of 24 "research essences" was released in 1981 on a more limited basis, along with a longer inventory of essences available for testing. Case study and clinical reports which have been received from practitioners have indicated that many people are deriving significant benefit from these new essences.

By sensitizing ourselves to what grows in our own "backyards" we can better appreciate Nature's gifts from other regions of the world, and become more attuned to the life force in Nature. Yet, in our emerging planetary culture we are not limited to our own particular corner of the world, although we find the roots of our relationship to the Earth in a particular region. The Bach remedies, developed primarily in rural England, have established a world-wide reputation for effectiveness. FES essences developed in California and other areas are now also gaining recognition throughout the world as valuable aids for spiritual and emotional growth.

The 38 remedies that Bach chose to leave to the world occupy a unique place in the history of flower essences, and we have a great respect for the courage and degree of evolvement it took to accomplish this work. Nonetheless, we should not let our admiration for Dr. Bach and his work obscure our vision of our own unique contributions for this age. Now that Dr. Bach has pioneered the way, it is for us to bring the knowledge and experience of the subtle qualities of flowers into the human community, making it part of our daily activity and awareness. We best honor pioneers such as Bach by considering their works as part of a living, growing, ever-evolving process of discovery.

If we examine the great spiritual traditions of the past,

we can see similar issues arising after the passing of the original teacher or way-shower. Those who truly understand the message of a Buddha or a Christ, for example, are those who take inspiration from the lives and teachings of these exemplers, and who discover and manifest the Buddha-nature and Christ-consciousness within themselves. Similarly, in such fields of knowledge as psychology, medicine and physics, those who have followed such great pioneers as Jung, Hahnemann or Einstein, have adapted, re-interpreted and expanded upon their foundational work.

Thus, those of us who draw inspiration from Dr. Bach's work, and who have experimented with preparing local essences, are not seeking to imitate Dr. Bach's work, or to duplicate his exact methodology. Rather, we seek to serve humanity in a way appropriate to our own spiritual guidance and evolvement, while participating in the collective evolutionary process of this "Aquarian Age."

In an earlier epoch it may have been necessary to guard spiritual knowledge with the authority of spiritual hierarchy and the protection of spiritual initiation. In this epoch we are now entering, however, it appears that such knowledge needs a wider dissemination so that it can be realized within the hearts and souls of many people, and not just a few initiates. This is necessary not only for evolution of human consciousness, but for the planet itself to fulfill its evolutionary destiny. The awakening of holistic and spiritual awareness in recent years has created a philosophical and cultural context in which the impulse of Dr. Bach's discoveries can be developed and applied on a wider scale.

Such an expanded work requires a high degree of responsibility and discipline. With the preparation of flower essences, we stress the importance of botanical observation, carefulness of procedure and, especially, the cultivation of proper attitude and attunement on the part of the essence-maker. We encourage practitioners to experiment with the new essences and report their clinical results to us. (Such feedback already has proved valuable as a source of empirical data.) We also envision a more extensive research program as appropriate institutes and universities make funds and resources available. Moreover, we encourage serious practitioners to enroll in the in-depth educational programs which are offered through the FES and the FETI, for we cannot overemphasize the importance of self-awareness and counseling skills in the successful application of the essences.

The Flower Essence Society, in association with the non-profit corporation Earth-Spirit, is a vehicle for developing this educational and research work. Although the Society serves the whole flower essence community, including many practitioners who combine the Bach and FES essences in their practices, it should be clearly understood that there is no institutional affiliation between the Bach Centre and the Flower Essence Society, and that the Bach Centre has no connection with the FES essences or any other flower essences besides the original 38 developed by Dr. Bach. And although some people use the term "Bach flowers" as a generic term for all flower essences, the Bach Centre has requested that the name "Bach" be reserved for only the 38 essences developed by Dr. Bach. We respect this request, and use the term "flower essences" as the generic reference. We recognize the desire of the Bach Centre to preserve the integrity of Dr. Bach's work, and urge others to support them in this endeavor.

All of us benefit when each of us is free to follow the path of service which best expresses the uniqueness of our individual capacity to serve. As our own work develops, we wish success to all others serving world healing.

Flower essences communicate Nature's message of unity, harmony and balance. Yet, no method can be more healing than the consciousness with which it is used. Let those of us who work with the life-affirming energies of the flower essences incorporate these qualities into our lives and relationships with each other. Let us attune to our greater unity of purpose within the one Spirit. Let us take to heart the words of Dr. Bach (describing the Beech essence), and be "more lenient, tolerant and understanding of the different way each individual and all things are working toward their own final perfection." (Bach, *The Twelve Healers*. London: C.W. Daniel Co., 1933, p. 23.)

Flower Essences:

Bach flower remedies:

The Dr. Bach Centre
Mt. Vernon, Sotwell,
Wallingford, Oxon. OX10 OPZ
England

The Ellon Company
P.O. Box 320
Woodmere, NY 11598 USA
(for USA & Canada)

FES (American) flower essences:

Flower Essence Services
P.O. Box 586
Nevada City, CA 95959 USA
(not associated with Bach Centre)

Qualities of the Bach Flower Essences

by Suzanne Garden

Quality: *inner quality or experience enhanced by the essence*
Pattern: *pattern of imbalance for which the essence is helpful*
Lesson: *life lesson which is the positive effect of the essence*

AGRIMONY *Agrimonia eupatoria*
Quality: Self-worth, self-acceptance; Joy.
Pattern: Separation between inner and outer world. Feeling that love and acceptance must be earned, fear of showing our inner selves.
Lesson: To love ourselves as we are, to allow ourselves to be fully seen by others, to allow our inner world to be openly expressed.

ASPEN *Populus tremula*
Quality: Courage to face the unknown.
Pattern: Fear of what is not measurable by the senses or the mind, fear that is subconscious enough to not be connected with its source, fear that is picked up from others and from environment.
Lesson: To face fear and not let it block us, to proceed in life even when we are afraid.

BEECH *Fagus sylvatica*
Quality: Self-definition, inner separation of self from environment; tolerance.
Pattern: Over-identification with the environment and people that are near; judgement and criticism of environment and others.
Lesson: To be sensitive to surroundings without being dependent on environment for well being; to be tolerant of self and others.

CENTAURY *Centaurium erythraea*
Quality: Service.
Pattern: Mentally defining service in terms of outward forms, especially in terms of giving to others.
Lesson: To know service as the energy and contact we bring to every aspect of our lives; to do what is necessary in terms of inner honesty to radiate an energy of love and presence, which may at times mean saying, "no, I can't do that for you now."

CERATO *Ceratostigma willmottianum*
Quality: Strength of inner knowing.
Pattern: Seeking validation through feedback from others, acting on our perceived projections of what others want us to do.
Lesson: To act on the basis of inner direction and knowing; to maintain an openness for feedback, while testing that feedback in terms of inner sense.

CHERRY PLUM *Prunus cerasifera*
Quality: Letting go (and letting God).
Pattern: Ego fear of losing control when shifting into intuitive directing of life; mental questioning and resistance to inner guidance.
Lesson: To let go of our limited personality perspective in order for our deeper direction to come through.

CHESTNUT BUD *Aesculus hippocastanum*
Quality: Vision.
Pattern: Getting stuck in the same recurring situations or behaviors.
Lesson: To "see" the lesson or meaning behind life's dramas so we can learn what we need to move on and not keep drawing the same lessons over and over again.

CHICORY *Cichorium intybus*
Quality: Interpersonal love.
Pattern: Giving love in order to receive it; adopting behaviors to get love and attention.
Lesson: To know the source of love within self; to feel Universal love; to love others unconditionally for the sake of loving.

CLEMATIS *Clematis vitalba*
Quality: Presence; being fully grounded.
Pattern: Not being fully conscious in moment-to-moment reality; resisting being on earth; not taking responsibility for the physical realities of life; living in the future.
Lesson: To realize that it is in being fully conscious and present in all aspects of our life that we contact and allow our deeper essence to flow.

CRAB APPLE *Malus sylvestris*
Quality: Cleansing and Purification.
Pattern: Having a need or desire for release and de-toxification on any or all levels (mental, emotional, physical, spiritual); feeling unclean.
Lesson: To accept process of cleansing as a necessary stage in the cycle of becoming clearer and more expanded in consciousness.

ELM *Ulums procera*
Quality: Perfection, Idealism.
Pattern: Having rigid concepts of perfection as something absolute and therefore unobtainable; for stress of trying to live up to idealized image of self.
Lesson: To understand the perfection that we are, without having to do anything; to incorporate our idealism into life in a realistic way.

GENTIAN *Gentianella amarella*
Quality: Courage to accept "what is."
Pattern: Creating negative realities through our negative projections; becoming discouraged and depressed by aspects of our lives.
Lesson: To take responsibility for creating our reality; to extract the positive from all life situations; to see life from a "win-win" perspective (what we're learning, how we're growing, etc.).

GORSE *Ulex europaeus*
Quality: Integration, especially of joy and sorrow.
Pattern: Seeing life as full of suffering, or else denying aspects of life in order to avoid pain; having feeling of despair.
Lesson: To go beyond the swing of positive-negative; to see the equality and validity of all aspects of life; to integrate personal pain (which allows us to stop suffering).

HEATHER *Calluna vulgaris*
Quality: Merging personal love and unconditional love.
Pattern: Focus on self love in terms of fulfilling personality needs.
Lesson: To see the personality as the flower of the soul; to work with personality needs of ourselves and others from the perspective of higher consciousness, so that we can love unconditionally through the vehicle of our personality.

HOLLY *Ilex aquifolium*
Quality: Bringing unconditional love through the emotions.
Pattern: Expression of "negative" emotions, such as anger, jealousy, hatred, etc.
Lesson: To recognize emotional energy as the energy of love; to see negative emotions as blocked or unclear love; to allow this love to flow freely and clearly.

HONEYSUCKLE *Lonicera caprifolium*
Quality: Presence, the ability to "be here now."
Pattern: Wanting to feel comfortable, and escape growth by somehow returning to a previous stage of development; often experienced as a longing for the past.
Lesson: To accept and affirm the present; to embrace the process of growth and change.

HORNBEAM *Carpinus betulus*
Quality: Strength to carry out personal intention.
Pattern: Feeling unable to cope with the daily, practical realities of life; feeling fatigue in the face of our personal responsibilities.
Lesson: To utilize our will in our daily life; to look at the balance between using personal will and allowing our lives to flow.

IMPATIENS *Impatiens glandulifera*
Quality: Patience.
Pattern: Being impatient, especially with others, but also with self; wanting to rush growth.
Lesson: To see the perfection of the process; to know that all life is progressing at its own unique rate.

LARCH *Larix decidua*
Quality: Self-confidence.
Pattern: Fear of failure; doubting our capabilities; allowing our fear to immobilize us.
Lesson: To realize that success and failure have no meaning in any absolute sense; that we are successful as long as we are growing (which we are doing whether we are conscious of it or not); to take action in our lives, even in the face of fear.

MIMULUS *Mimulus guttatus*
Quality: Freedom within form.
Pattern: Fear of limitation and separation; fear of being trapped in form; fear of anything that can be identified; fear of being on Earth.
Lesson: To accept the forms of life and work within them; to accept physical reality, to know that we are not limited by it.

MUSTARD *Sinapis arvensis*
Quality: Faith.
Pattern: Gloom, depression, melancholia, sadness.
Lesson: To go forward in times of darkness with the faith that this inevitably leads to greater light; to experience the process of facing our shadow as a positive and essential part of our evolution in consciousness.

OAK *Quercus robur*
Quality: Surrender.
Pattern: Fighting and struggling with our lives and process; believing that we must struggle in order to grow.
Lesson: To understand that as long as we're fighting we're inhibiting, rather than facilitating our growth; to allow ourselves to accept the flow of our lives, realizing that we will be presented with all that we need to take our next steps.

OLIVE *Olea europea*
Quality: Regeneration.
Pattern: Exhaustion on all levels, especially inner ones; psychic exhaustion from having given too much of ourselves.
Lesson: To tap into our unlimited energy source; to let go of the thought that we are giving of our own energy; to recognize realistically what we can do without becoming drained.

PINE *Pinus sylvestris*
Quality: Responsibility.
Pattern: Thinking of responsibility in terms of what we "should" do; feeling overwhelmed by a sense of duty and obligation; feeling guilt and self-blame.
Lesson: To realize that responsibility is our ability to re-spond, or make meaningful contact, with our lives; to allow ourselves the freedom to be present with our lives without the thought forms of what we "ought" to be doing; to release our need to control and direct life.

RED CHESTNUT *Aesculus carnea*
Quality: Inner sensitivity; ability to connect with others on an inner level.
Pattern: Tendency to become psychically enmeshed in the karma and patterns of others; to project our emotions and thoughts onto others.
Lesson: To disassociate from our individual, personality self. To realize our greater identity.

ROCK ROSE *Helianthemum nummularium*
Quality: Transcendence.
Pattern: Extreme terror, panic, and fear; often fear, either consciously or unconsciously of losing life, or losing identity.
Lesson: To disassociate from our individual, personality self. To realize our greater identity.

ROCK WATER (solarized spring water)
Quality: Discipline.
Pattern: Extreme self-discipline or self-denial; martyrdom; imposing ideas of discipline on ourselves.
Lesson: To experience the discipline inherent within ourselves and all of life; to trust this greater innate order and rhythm of life; to let go of the need to be mentally strict with ourselves.

SCLERANTHUS *Scleranthus annuus*
Quality: Balance; stability.
Pattern: Wavering between two polarities (mentally or emotionally); facing a decision between two choices.
Lesson: To make decisions from as clear a perspective as possible; to see that sometimes there is no need to choose, but rather that seeming opposites can be integrated into a greater whole; to find a balance point in all areas of our lives.

STAR OF BETHLEHEM *Ornithogalum umbellatum*
Quality: Peace.
Pattern: Shock or trauma on a physical, emotional, or mental level.
Lesson: To let shocks pass through us, without creating blocks or tensions; to maintain inner peace even in outward chaos; to release the effects of previous shocks and traumas, including birth trauma.

SWEET CHESTNUT *Castanea sativa*
Quality: Transformation.
Pattern: Feeling stretched beyond all capabilities and definitions.
Lesson: To experience time of tremendous growth in consciousness, without resisting or feeling shattered; to go beyond definitions and boundaries.

VERVAIN *Verbena officinalis*
Quality: Will.
Pattern: Using personal will and personal ideology to define the nature of reality; seeking to convert others to personal belief system.
Lesson: To align personal will with Universal will; to let others actualize themselves according to their own direction; to activate the energy of will without the limitations of personal beliefs.

VINE *Vitis vinifera*
Quality: Authority.
Pattern: Extending personal authority to include authority over others; seeking to be "helpful" to others by directing their activities.
Lesson: To understand that true authority transcends the individual; to allow each person to contact that deeper authority within.

WALNUT *Juglans regia*
Quality: Freedom; protection.
Pattern: Influenced by outside forces, such as other people, the environment, society, our own patterning; being open to thoughts and emotions projected on us by others, or pervading our environment.
Lesson: To shut our external forces and clearly hear our own inner voice; to be free to follow our own unique direction in life.

WATER VIOLET *Hottonia palustris*
Quality: Communion with others.
Pattern: Feeling separate or aloof from other people, although very strong and centered within self.
Lesson: To bring inner essence into relationship with others; to see our communion with other people as essential for self-fulfillment.

WHITE CHESTNUT *Aesculus hippocastanum*
Quality: Clarity of mind.
Pattern: Mental chatter; unnecessary thoughts.
Lesson: To empty the mind so that our creative and intuitive faculties can operate; to experience a dynamic stillness of mind.

WILD OAT *Bromus ramosus*
Quality: Life purpose.
Pattern: Lack of focus; inability to express purpose in life, or to align purpose and livelihood.
Lesson: To integrate self energies in order to sense, and then actualize soul purpose in life.

WILD ROSE *Rosa canina*
Quality: Participation in life.
Pattern: Apathy, resignation to be the effect, rather than the cause of one's reality.
Lesson: To accept creative power in life; to dynamically interact with all aspects of life in order to responsibly express ourselves in the world.

WILLOW *Salix alba* ssp. *vitellina*
Quality: Owning creative power of thought.
Pattern: Creating negative reality, and then blaming outside forces.
Lesson: To acknowledge our responsibility for the situations in our life; to create the most positive reality possible.

RESCUE REMEDY (a composite of Cherry Plum, Clematis, Impatiens, Rock Rose and Star of Bethlehem)
Quality: Emergency.
Pattern: All aspects of emergency as crisis; accidents, physical ailments, emotional upsets, etc.
Lesson: To understand and facilitate the ongoing process of emergence in our lives; to smooth out the highs and lows that can hinder growth and development.

WILD ROSE *Rosa canina*

Qualities of the FES Flower Essences

by Richard Katz

COMMON AND BOTANICAL NAMES	LIFE LESSONS AND INNER QUALITIES	PATTERNS OF IMBALANCE
BLACKBERRY *Rubus ursinus*	conscious manifestation, creative power of thought.	directing thoughts to fear, conflict, limitation; inertia, feeling stuck.
BORAGE *Borago officinalis*	cheerful courage, confidence and ease in facing danger and challenge.	feeling disheartened, discouraged.
CALIFORNIA POPPY *Eschscholzia californica*	psychic opening, spiritual balance, integration of past life abilities and knowledge, spiritual sight.	blockages of creativity and intuition, externalization of spiritual goals.
CHAMOMILE *Anthemis cotula*	inner harmony and calm, mental clarity, meditative receptivity, emotional objectivity.	nervous, confused, difficulty relaxing or sleeping, emotionally upset.
DILL *Anethum graveolens*	assimilation of experience.	feeling overwhelmed, over-stimulated by the pace of life.
FUCHSIA *Fuchsia hybrida*	experiencing and understanding blocked emotions.	mental tension, repressed emotions.
IRIS *Iris douglasiana*	transcending limitation, identification with the universal, external; creative and artistic expression.	feeling frustrated, limited, inadequate.
MADIA *Madia elegans*	concentration, focus, follow-through, attention to detail, clarity.	tendency to be easily distracted, over-extended.
MANZANITA *Arctostaphylos viscida*	groundedness, embodiment, knowing the body as "the temple of the spirit."	flighty, ungrounded, ambivalent about being in the body.
MORNING GLORY *Ipomoea purpurea*	balance and toning of vital energy, alertness, viewing life from a fresh perspective.	restlessness, jitteriness, compulsive habits and addictions, extremes of energy.
NASTURTIUM *Tropaeolum majus*	earthy expressiveness, vitality.	over-intellectuality, lacking vitality, lethargy.
PENSTEMON *Penstemon davidsonii*	inner strength through adverse circumstances; resolving conflicts in relationships.	self-doubt, feeling overwhelmed by challenges, adversity, conflict.
PINK YARROW *Achillea millefolium* var. *rubra*	emotional strength and self-protection.	emotional vulnerability.

RED CLOVER *Trifolium pratense*	centeredness and balance, non-susceptibility to emotionalism/hysteria.	being swept up in mass emotionalism, hysteria, fear, panic.
SAGEBRUSH *Artemisia tridentata*	being true to one's higher-self, purification of what is inessential.	overly influenced by others, false identification with self-image.
SCARLET MONKEYFLOWER *Mimulus cardinalis*	freedom of emotional expression; integration of shadow side of self, of emotional energy.	emotional repression, fear of powerful emotion.
SCOTCH BROOM *Cytisus scoparius*	motivation, perserverance, faith; acceptance of difficulties as opportunities.	despair, pessimism, alienation, feeling "what's the use."
SELF-HEAL *Prunella vulgaris*	self-healing power of self-acceptance and self-trust; being nourished by life energy.	self-doubt, confusion, lack of self-love.
SHASTA DAISY *Chysanthemum maximum*	self-actualizing, synthesis of knowledge; mental organization.	scattered seeking, unintegrated knowledge.
STAR TULIP *Calochortus tolmiei*	spiritual and psychic opening; sensitivity, receptivity, attunement to the subtle realm.	fear and blockage of psychic sensitivity and spiritual receptivity.
STICKY MONKEYFLOWER *Mimulus aurantiacus*	awareness of sexual issues, integration of sexual and emotional energies; balance in sexual expression.	fear of intimacy, confusion about sexuality.
SUNFLOWER *Helianthus annuus*	harmonizing ego with higher self; balancing of masculine aspect of self.	egotistical attitude, or fear of being egotistical; conflict about paternal parental image.
SWEET PEA *Lathyrus latifolus*	social responsiveness and responsibility; rootedness, present-time awareness.	anti-social attitudes, conflict with family or friends, fear of commitment; not being present.
YARROW *Achillea millefolium* var. *borealis* var. *lanulosa*	protection from harm by the strength of one's inner light.	vulnerability to psychic or emotional negativity, or to harmful environmental influences or energies.

Please Note:

These descriptions of flower essences and their uses are offered as suggestions for guiding your own explorations and research. They are based on a vibrational attunement with the flowers, information received intuitively and psychically, and reports from individuals using these essences.

Each person interprets his/her experiences with flower essences through a unique life history and perspective. We encourage you to freely adapt these generalized descriptions to language of your own understanding. We also request feedback on your experiences with the essences to assist our evolving understanding of their uses and effects.

Flower Essence Journal Contributors

PAMELA BEESLEY is a free-lance graphic artist and illustrator who lives and works in Nevada City, California.

NIKI BROYLES has been a resident of Oakland, California for 30 years, and has been painting for 15 years. She is a wife and mother and includes among her interests metaphysics, mysticism and meditation.

CATALINA is an artist living in Nevada City, California. She is the designer of the Flower Essence Society Iris logo.

ENTÉRA resides in Porterville, California, where she pursues a synthesis of literary, healing and fine arts in her work, as well as sharing the gift of creativity through teaching. She is also a partner in the newly-opened Renaissance Center, the first new-age resource/holistic health center in the area.

SUZANNE GARDEN is founder and director of the Flower Essence Training Institute offering in-depth educational programs for flower essence practitioners. A former member of the Findhorn Foundation in Scotland, and a former director of the Sirius community is Massachusetts, Suzanne now resides in Northampton, Massachusetts, where she is a counselor and teacher.

PENELOPE HOBLIN is an artist living in Windsor, Vermont, who seeks to blend her gifts of music, color, light and flowers into a unified message of divine celebration.

PATRICIA KAMINSKI is co-director of the Flower Essence Society and president of Earth-Spirit. Following childhood on a farm in rural Nebraska, she earned a B.A. in Women Studies at the University of Nebraska-Lincoln and went on to work as a social activist and legislative researcher. In 1979 she completed a three-year residence in a spiritual community, studying solar energy. It was here that she began experimenting with solar water infused with herbs and crystals.

RICHARD KATZ is the founder and co-director of the Flower Essence Society. He has spent the last fourteen years exploring humanistic and transpersonal psychology; meditation and yoga; nutrition, herbology, gardening, Eastern, Western and Native American spiritual traditions. He has pioneered the development of new flower essences from California and other areas.

STEVE KOKE is a free-lance photographer and astrologer in Nevada County, California.

RICHARD LAMM grew up in Philadelphia, Pennsylvania, and worked for some years in chemical research and teaching mathematics. He left America to follow an artistic career in Europe, where he was a professional artist for twelve years. He traveled and studied yoga meditation and astrology, and became resident astrologer-teacher at the Kosmos Meditation Center in Amsterdam where he lectured and led groups for eight years. He now lives on the island of Ibiza, Spain, and travels and lectures in the USA and Europe. He has worked with flower essences for eight years, and includes them as part of his healing/counseling work.

LARRY MILLER is a photographer and co-owner of Local Color photographic studios in Grass Valley, California.

ELLEN SCHAEFER PERCHONOCK, Ph.D. is a teacher, counselor, communicator and dancer now living in Montague, Massachusetts, after many years in Amsterdam. She works in the areas of astrology and natural healing, including flower essences, and does typing/editorial work to make a living.

MICHAEL PINTER is a photographer and co-owner of Local Color photographic studios in Grass Valley, California.

RICHARD PITCAIRN, D.V.M., Ph.D. is a holistic veterinarian practicing in the Santa Cruz, California area. He writes the column "Your Healthy Pet" for *Prevention* magazine, and has written a book, *The Complete Book of Natural Pet Care: Dogs and Cats.*

DAVID SHERROD is an artist from California's Sierra mountains who now makes his home in Sedona, Arizona. He has been an illustrator for the State Park System and a magazine book illustrator. His recent art is dedicated to communicating the Native American experience.

DAVID SIEGLER is a free-lance phtographer, masseur and holistic practitioner using flower essences in Mill Valley, California.

DAVID SPANGLER, whose writing is excerpted in this issue, is one of the leading thinkers of new age consciousness. He was a leading member of the Findhorn community for three years, and helped found and direct the Lorian Association in the USA. He is a prolific author and song-writer.

MAITREYA STILLWATER is a musician and artist living in Marin County, California. He is co-director of Heavensong, a ministry of healing music, and has produced three cassette tapes.

JOHN TINGLEY is an artist, architect, designer and writer living and working in New York City. His work includes personal mandalas for meditation and the recognition of inner energies, logos for personal or business use, architectural design, "mystical spaces and abstract interpretation."

DARRELL WRIGHT is a self-taught botanist of nine years' experience who lives and works in the San Francisco Bay Area. He is preparing an update of Marin County, California flora, and has been published in *Madrono*, the journal of the California Botanical Society. He is the chief botanical consultant for the Flower Essence Society.

The Flower Essence Society expresses its appreciation for the support of the following members:

Lifetime members:

Barbara Miller
Suzannah Schroll

Supporting members:

Jim & Isara Drummond
Sara Proctor Esswein
Barry Gordon
Shari Nelberg
Helen Parnell
Bleema Pressman
Lyn Rollins
Victoria Weaver

Organizational members:

Marjorie S. Alseth
45-675 Apuakea St.
Kaneohe, HI 96744

Abram Ber, MD
3134 N. 7th St.
Phoenix, AZ 85014

The Center of Light
P.O. Box 540
Great Barrington, MA 01230

Peter S. Howe
27 Grove St.
Scituate, MA 02066

Klara-Simpla
10 Main St.
Wilmington, VT 05363

Dr. Amrit Singh Khalsa
958 San Pablo Ave.
Albany, CA 94706

Li Chiropractic Healing Arts Center
2067 Broadway, Suite 70
New York, NY 10023

Light Wave Enterprises
3151 Wilshire Blvd.
Los Angeles, CA 90010

Lisa's Beauty Salon
1047 S. Blvd.
Oak Park, IL 60302

Massage Therapy Training Institute
1732 W. Main St.
Houston, TX 77098

Amarisia Munn
853 Calero Ave.
San Jose, CA 95123

Nature's Products
20020 Conant
Detroit, MI 48234

New West Natural Foods
970 Market St.
San Francisco, CA 94102

Polarity Center Boston
41 Dunster Rd.
Jamaica Plain, MA 02130

The Rainbow Bridge
125 Lakeview Ave.
West Palm Beach, FL 33401

Rainbow General Store
3139 16th St.
San Francisco, CA 94103

Real Food Company #2
3939 24th St.
San Francisco, CA 94114

Real Food Store
30922 Hilltop Dr.
Evergreen, CO 80439

Safe Space
c/o B. Fahr & S. Sun
260 San Jose Ave., #306
San Francisco, CA 94110

Wholistic Health Center
803 4th St.
San Rafael, CA 94901

Wholistic Health Center
Cedars Sinai Medical
Office Towers
8631 W. Third St., Suite 1110 E
Los Angeles, CA 90048

The Yoga Center, Inc.
P.O. Box 1589
Pittsfield, MA 01201

Don't miss our back issues!

Issue #1:
Welcome to the Eighties
Flower Essences: Natural Health Catalysts
Lessons of the Bach Flower Essences
Intuitional Readings in Flower Essence Consciousness
Bach Flower Essence Research
Living with the Flowers, I
Botany of the Bach Flowers, I
Book Review: *Look at a Flower*
Holly and the Holy Spirit
Master's Essences
Exploring California Flower Essence, I
Preparing Your Own Flower Essences

For each copy, send $3 (plus tax and shipping) to:

The Flower Essence Society
P.O. Box 459, Nevada City, CA 95959

Issue #2:
The Spirit of Cooperation
Flower Essences: A Counselor's Perspective
Radiesthesia: A Tool of Intuitive Perception
Flower Essence Affirmations
Bach Flower Essence Research: Interview
Botany of the Bach Flowers, II
Living with the Flowers: Natural Flower Foods
Exploring California Flower Essences, II

Issue #3
Science and Spirit
Flower Essences and Imagery
Flower Essence Case Studies
Personal and Planetary Evolution
Affirmation-Response Techniques
Botany of the Bach Flowers, III
More Natural Flower Foods
Exploring California Flower Essences, III

THE FLOWER ESSENCE SOCIETY

P.O. Box 459, Nevada City, CA 95959   (916) 265-9163

Co-directors: Richard Katz, Patricia Kaminski   Botanical consultant: Darrell Wright

The Flower Essence Society was organized in 1979 by Richard Katz, and works in association with Earth-Spirit, a non-profit educational and research organization dedicated "to promoting the harmony of humankind with the living Earth and all its forms of life, and with the Spirit which is the source of life." The unique aims of the Flower Essence Society are to create a world-wide communications network among the many practitioners and others using flower essences, to encourage scientific and intuitive investigation of the essences, and to create a land center for flower essence educational and research programs. The Society recognizes the pioneering work of Dr. Edward Bach in the 1930's in England in developing the Bach Flower Essences, and it is actively researching important new flower essences developed in recent years in California and other regions of the world. In this age of intense transformation, we call for a new awareness of flower essences as a significant tool for personal and planetary evolution. To those who share our vision, we offer our services and assistance. We invite your participation and support of this work through your Flower Essence Society membership.

Flower Essence Society members receive periodic newsletters (sent only to members) with articles, artwork, case studies, announcements of classes, new essences and other research, and member notices. In addition, members receive the next issue of the *Flower Essence Journal* (now published annually) and the Members' Directory (arranged geographically with short descriptions).

Individual Membership is available to anyone wishing to support the FES and participate in the FES network.

Organizational Membership is available to centers, clinics, groups, stores and others who wish an organizational affiliation with the FES. Organizational members receive two copies of Newsletters, Journals and Directories, and are given special listings in the *Journal* and Directory.

Those wishing to contribute substantial financial support to the work of the FES may choose one of the following memberships:

Supporting Membership
Lifetime Membership

As a gesture of appreciation, supporting and lifetime members will be acknowledged in the *Journal*, and will be offered the assistance of the FES staff in any special project they may choose involving flower essences.